A
PERFECT
10

ALSO BY HEATHER LAND

I Ain't Doin' It

A PERFECT 10

*The Truth About Things
I'm Not and Never Will Be*

HEATHER LAND

with Heather Lenard

HOWARD BOOKS

ATRIA

New York London Toronto Sydney New Delhi

HOWARD
BOOKS

ATRIA

An Imprint of Simon & Schuster, Inc.
1230 Avenue of the Americas
New York, NY 10020

First Howard Books/Atria Paperback edition May 2021

HOWARD BOOKS/**ATRIA** PAPERBACK and colophon
are trademarks of Simon & Schuster, Inc.

For information about special discounts for bulk purchases, please contact Simon
& Schuster Special Sales at 1-866-506-1949 or business@simonandschuster.com.

The Simon & Schuster Speakers Bureau can bring authors to your live event. For
more information or to book an event, contact the Simon & Schuster Speakers
Bureau at 1-866-248-3049 or visit our website at www.simonspeakers.com.

Manufactured in the United States of America

10 9 8 7 6 5 4 3 2 1

Library of Congress Cataloging-in-Publication Data

Names: Land, Heather, author.
Title: A perfect 10 : the truth about things I'm not and never will be / Heather Land.
Other titles: Perfect ten
Description: First Howard Books hardcover edition. | New York : Howard Books,
2020. | Identifiers: LCCN 2019059972 (print) | LCCN 2019059973 (ebook) |
ISBN 9781982104184 (hardcover) | ISBN 9781982104207 (ebook)
Subjects: LCSH: Land, Heather. | Comedians—United States—Biography. |
Conduct of life—Humor.
Classification: LCC PN2287.L2465 A3 2020 (print) | LCC PN2287.L2465
(ebook) | DDC 818/.602—dc23
LC record available at https://lccn.loc.gov/2019059972
LC ebook record available at https://lccn.loc.gov/2019059973

ISBN 978-1-9821-0418-4
ISBN 978-1-9821-0419-1 (pbk)
ISBN 978-1-9821-0420-7 (ebook)

CONTENTS

CONTENTS

INTRODUCTION

Have you ever been in the ocean and looked around to realize you are a little too far away from where you started? And the harder you kick, the farther away the swell takes you? Let's get one thing straight. I have known swells. Mostly water retention. Like my ankles that one time I gained eighty pounds during my second pregnancy. I looked like I had swallowed eighty pounds of Little Debbie Star Crunch. Because I had. The swelling was off the charts. My nose just blended in with my cheeks; there was no distinction. I was unrecognizable. I have known some swelling.

And we all know that monthly water-retention swelling, don't we, girls? Help it. I have known heat and humidity all my stinkin' life in the South. The swelling (and boob sweat) that comes with summer in the South ain't no joke.

How about that one time I went on a retreat with my (ex-)in-laws and (ex-)husband and got so nervous that my body reacted in a totally crazy way. There was no other explanation for it but a good ol' case of the nerves. My bottom lip was so swollen that I couldn't talk or close my mouth. I made swole-up Will Smith in *Hitch* look like a supermodel. I had to hide out—forced to stay indoors alone. Which, let's be honest, was my goal in the first place. I set my sights on achieving that goal, and I crushed it!

I wish I was using the adjective "swell" like they did on *The Brady Bunch* when I describe past seasons of my life. As in "Everything about my marriage was swell." Or "Dating in my forties is going swell." Stop right there. "Swell" could never describe either of those seasons of my life. That's not the kind of swelling I am talking about.

There were times I didn't think I would be able to stay on top of the water. Kicking my legs, gasping for air, inhaling large gulps of water into my throat. Surely I would die out there. Surely no one would find me. There was so much rocky water that no ship would dare set sail. And I was floating in it. No one would choose that course. No one would chart my course for me. I had to do it myself.

Isn't that how life works? Being knocked around by waves that you can see coming a mile away? It's never the immediate storms around us. It's the waves that are a result of distant weather. Distant choices. Past warning signs that we overlooked. Old heart wounds that went unattended. Unconscious beliefs and biases that rear their ugly heads when you need them not to.

Most of you probably already know this from my first book. Oh, you didn't read it? Shame on you. *It can still be purchased where books are sold.* This *I Ain't Doin It* journey has taken me on a wild ride. What started as a dare has turned out to be the stupidest, most pivotal time of my life. I was perfectly content for the time being, sitting behind my desk from eight to five. I had finally recovered from divorce and was finding my sea legs when I posted my first sarcastic video to social media. The viral onslaught that overtook my life and forced me to make the choice between my desk job and a career in comedy was something I never saw coming.

Besides all that, posting that first video on Facebook while I was a single fortysomething was not the ideal way to enter the online-dating scene. But as we all know, social media is the great equalizer. It takes a nobody (me) and thrusts them into a world of entertainment. What in the actual h-e-double-hockey-sticks just happened? I went from sitting down at a desk to doing stand-up faster than you can say "Jeff Foxworthy."

Sounds easy, right? Sounds like it was handed to me on a silver platter. Well, I do recognize that comedians and writers work their entire lives for an opportunity like the one I have been given. I acknowledge that, and I am incredibly thankful.

I would also like to acknowledge that there is no way I would have signed up for this gig. I would have been petrified to talk into a microphone for more than one minute. Sing? Oh, yeah, if you want me to sing, I am your girl. But tell jokes? Naw, I am good.

I barely knew how to build a life as a single mom to two teenagers, much less as a traveling, entertaining single mom. I had no idea what I would talk about on a stage. I am just a simple, small-town Southern girl who grew up with some turmoil in her life, addiction in her home, poor life choices, deeply religious roots, and utter disdain for stupid people and Walmart. Move along, folks, nothing to see here. Just me trying to joke my way through life to avoid a permanent come-apart.

So that's when I decided to get up onstage and air out my dirty laundry. Because that's what we all want: to hear other people's real-life stories that make us feel human. We all want to know that someone survived the swell. We want to know that it's OK to laugh. Life is serious enough. And personally, I am offended by it.

This crazy ride has helped me shed some shackles I did not know I had. It's forced me to acknowledge the crap that I haven't wanted to deal with. It's forced me to get over myself. And I had to get over you—your opinion of me. I had to face comments from strangers who voiced their thoughts about my life and my humor. I had to work through my people-pleasing upbringing and decide who grown-up Heather was going to be.

I have made a life off of four little words: *I Ain't Doin' It. Well, technically, that is five words, but my Ivy League grammar allows me to shorten my flagship phrase to only four words by using a contraction.* Well, the words on the pages ahead are going to take you on a journey not about the things I ain't doin' but about the things I have done. *CrossFit is still not on that list.*

So in this book, I want to share some of the things I learned trying to stay afloat. Things that have me fed up, lies that I have believed for too long, things that are tied to shame and discouragement, things that prevent me from loving people around me, and things that make me human. Hopefully, some of my own near-(emotional-)death experiences will help keep you from drowning, and hopefully, my willingness to laugh at my own life will help you realize that you don't have to be a perfect 10.

1

GROWING UP NORMAL

Lightning bugs, bare feet, and watermelon. Hometown stores where everyone knows your name and anyone can discipline you in the absence of your mama. A childhood in the South looks and feels very Norman Rockwell, doesn't it? Like pasty-white kids just kicking rocks and hanging out at the local barbershop with their lunch pails in tow.

The South taught me a lot about hospitality and generosity and simply taking care of folks regardless of their status. I was fortunate to grow up in a small town in West Tennessee where family and church were at the center of everything I knew. Church twice on Sundays and a Wednesday-night supper before prayer meeting every stinking week of my life. I am a product of all things Southern and holy with barbecue sauce on top.

In the South, we also learn to laugh at ourselves. I mean, come on. How could we not? You've seen us online. The world is not laughing with us. I am convinced that the majority of faces seen on the People of Walmart website are from my hometown alone.

There's not a whole lot to do in the Deep South. You either ride around to the Sonic or you ride around on the Tilt-A-Whirl at the County Fair. You can either enter 4-H or enter a pageant—show off your hogs or show off your daughter. You either boot-scootin' boogie or you bootleg. We love yard sales and baby showers. We serve bologna sandwiches at wedding receptions, and we put sugar in everything and wonder why we are fat.

We draw out our words, add syllables for inflection and throw in some clever phraseology for dramatic effect. For example, you have the option to say "She has buck teeth," or you can dress it up with "Bless her heart, she could eat an apple through a picket fence." We are going to find words that are meaner than a junkyard dog, dress them up, and use them to confuse the outsiders. They'll never know what hit them.

We're living in high cotton.

Drunker than Cooter Brown.

She was madder than a wet hen.

You can't make a silk purse out of a sow's ear.

She is happier than a pig in slop.

He thinks the sun comes up just to hear him crow.

That's about as useful as tits on a bull.

He's got enough money to burn a wet mule.

I haven't seen you since ol' Buck was a little calf.

We are going to use all the words, way too many words, to get our point across. We are going to talk about people while trying to make it sound polite. Just because we talk slow doesn't mean we are stupid. Sure, I've got a charming drawl, but I could also have a master's in biochemical engineering with a pastry chef undergrad. You'll never know, because we all sound alike, but you'd be a fool to underestimate us.

Growing up, I thought the ice cream truck was just for me. The ice cream man knew my name and my parents' names, and he had my order memorized. Because most of our parents grew up working in some type of agriculture, I spent my summers shelling peas. I learned the proper ratio for my grandmother's iron-skillet buttermilk biscuits when I was too young to even read the recipe card. We learned how to properly set a table, because, of course, our family ate dinner together every evening. We learned to appreciate a one-dish meal that a can of cream of chicken soup melded together. The slam of a screen door and the squeak of a porch swing are the background music to my soul.

We learned how to be frugal. At the dinner table, we passed a dishcloth to wipe our mouths because paper towels were just too expensive. And every good Southerner knows what the Sears, Roebuck catalog is good for . . . toilet paper! Wad it up, get it soft, and *voilà*! That catalog from the Avon lady was our fly swatter (pronounced "floss-water").

Growing up in the South provides an education for every part of life. We learned how to spot a killer snake in an instant—"Red on black, venom lack; red on yellow, kill a fellow" has saved the life of some poor soul you know. We learned how to tell stories, how to tell the truth, how to flatter, and how to cherish family. We know how to strike up conversations with strangers, because they could very well be someone's cousin—and you'll never know unless you talk to them. We learned to write thank-yous at a young age, for everything. We make friends fast, and we make friends forever. We grew up with Friday-night football shutting the town down and crosstown rivalries.

We knew how to make our own fun, use our imagination, and play pretend on family farms and in the woods. We learned how to be good stewards of what we own. Our family is the quirky cast of our childhood stories, including all the cousins. Everyone in a Southern family chips in to help—with homework, with transportation, with grocery shopping.

Southerners are also polite. Polite to a fault. Toxically at times. (Is that even a word?) Especially Southern women. We learn to please, we learn to agree, and we learn to say "Yes, sir." Take the culture of politeness and throw in religion, and what you have there is a whole lot of passive-aggressive "bless her hearts" and people who may not have the tools to say what they mean, much less fight for what they want out of life.

When I lived in Colorado, people would laugh at things I said that weren't funny at all. But the accent and subtle nuances in my stories made everything funny—and the fact that no one west of the Mississippi has ever heard of buying boiled peanuts from a gas station. I hate it for them, because they are truly missing out. Our finest delicacies come from gas stations up the road, and we are OK with that. When we stop at the QuikStop gas station for some food, do not be misled. There's no such thing as a "quick trip" anywhere in a small Southern town. I'll see my third-grade teacher's nephew at the gas pump and spend a full half hour listening to him describe his recent ingrown toenail. People who aren't from around here think we are a total alien invasion.

Not only did I grow up in the South, but I also grew up as an only child. Which means my parents and my granny were my best friends until I was old enough to drive and get the heck outta there. They were my only source of information and entertainment during my most impressionable years.

I didn't have an older sister (or brother) who was bringing crucial information back home from life on the streets. That valuable info like the best way to get that perfect shade of blue eye shadow that a sister learned on the public-school bus. Or the brother who learned about the birds and the bees from the nudie magazine in the boys' locker room. None of that. It was me, Bud, and Glenda. And Granny. *God rest Granny's beautiful soul.*

Allow me to share some weird things about my family. I grew up with a pay phone in my house. Yes, a pay phone from the local telephone company. Like the kind you would see on the sidewalk down at the dollar store in the 1990s. Mounted on the wall. Coins were required to make a phone call. *I will pause and let you pick your jaw up off the floor.*

When my parents were first married (and broke as a joke), my mom was homesick and kept calling her sister long-distance and talking for hours on end. I don't know if you remember the days before cell phones, but let me remind you, calls out of your area code cost money per minute. Well, Bud didn't like the phone bill getting so out of control every month. So after several threats, he called down to South Central Bell and asked if they could install a pay phone in our residence. Of course, it went something like this: "Gosh, I don't think we have ever gotten a request like that. But I suppose we can make that happen, Mr. Cole." And that is how it happened. I used a pay phone for years in my own home. When my friends were getting their own landlines and those tacky see-through phones, I had to pull up a stool with a jar of coins to talk to my friends. It was almost like a parental version of bullying.

My audience often asks, "Have you always been funny?" "Are your parents funny?" or "Did you know you were funny when you were a kid?" This always stumps me, because I am shocked that people want to know the Heather before the *I Ain't Doin' It* Heather. And there's nothing much different to report. I have always been an entertainer singing into a hairbrush. This kid was a hit with adults. I could own a room of my parents' friends. Same goes at church. I learned at a very young age how to behave onstage. How to move and position myself to emulate the behavior of evangelists across the globe. My dimples earned me lots of brownie points. Not so much my lazy eye, though.

I suppose my parents do have a sense of humor. Like the one time we were on a flight that was landing in Tennessee. We were approaching the runway when my mother regained cell phone service. She called Granny and said, "Our plane is going down. I just wanted to call you and tell you I love you." She thought it was the funniest thing she had ever said. *Really, Mom?* She is still laughing about it to this day.

Glenda, my petite mom, always has her "face on" and hair set in place. Always. *See definition of a Southern woman.* Except she loves mowing the grass on her riding mower. She loves it so much we have to threaten to cut her wires so she won't get heatstroke. Glenda has to explain to my dad when I am making a joke. "Bud, she's being funny. That was a joke, Bud."

My parents are very proud of me as an adult, but let's be honest here. I still don't think they believe I am funny enough to make a living doing any of this *I Ain't Doin' It* stuff. They would possibly be happier if I worked as a drive-thru teller at the local bank and volunteered in the church nursery every Sunday. It would make everyone a little more comfortable if I was a little more status quo. A little more inside the box, less outside the box. I haven't always been like this. I have walked the line for a very, very long time.

Bud has also greatly contributed to my stand-up material. "Come on over and see how I am spending your inheritance." Normally, we don't chitchat on the phone, but that was a conversation I didn't mind having. He had bought a pontoon boat that looked like a Clampett hand-me-down. It looked like a camper that had its roof knocked off by an interstate overpass. That banged-up tin can looked like it was sitting atop two rusty giant bananas. Oh, so you're telling me that my inheritance is $248? I hate to tell you, Bud, but it's gonna take more than that to put your tail in a nursing home. Also, Bud, I appreciate the comedic effort, but you are going to have to work on your delivery.

I didn't develop my parents' "sharp wit" until much later in life. As a young girl, I was actually an anxious little thing. I can't tell you how many times I spilled chocolate milk on my clothes at school, and the anxiety that followed always resulted in me faking an illness so I could go home. Concern for everyone around me kept my mind and body in a constant state of panic.

During my growing-up years, like every child, I had a need for all to be right in my world. I grew to be adaptable and didn't know anything but my own "normal." I longed for an equilibrium that kept everyone and everything feeling right. I needed desperately for this "thing," this semblance of normalcy, to be real and authentic. I was a people pleaser. I wanted to keep the peace. Fix it. Hide it. Compromise to make sure everything and everyone stayed OK. I needed this facade to be more than smoke and mirrors, but it wasn't. And deep in my gut, I knew it. Something wasn't right. I had to grow up pretty fast, and I had to take care of matters that should have never been mine to take care of. What I experienced as a young girl, I later realized, was far from normal.

When you are a kid, you don't have the tools to manage grown-up situations. And you don't get a choice. You are dealt a hand, and you just have to learn how to play. And you learn to cope. You eventually learn how the world works through a not-so-rosy lens.

I was a dream kid. I was every youth minister's prized possession. And that's how I hid in church. I grew up knowing how to perform for God and everybody else around me. I could hide in people's approval of me. I could hide behind my keyboard on a stage singing about Jesus. I could hide in my small Southern town. I could eventually hide in pursuing marriage and motherhood. All very noble and worthwhile things. All the things that provided protection and shelter to this ol' girl. I was sent out into this world with a very naive heart and a toolbox for fixing people.

I found myself in situations and relationships that weren't life-giving, they were life-sucking, and I didn't know how to get out. I felt like there was no future for me. I found myself caring about others' lives more than they did. I found myself accommodating others' tempers and narcissism. I found myself justifying emotional abuse and manipulation. I don't know if it came from being an only child or growing up in the South, or if it is just my God-given temperament. But I do know that I am not alone in this. I think we all spend most of our adult years trying to understand our childhood so that we can explain our weaknesses and quirks. Lord knows I have enough of them.

I have met many women who identify with this in one way or another. We work hard at pleasing everyone and keeping everyone at peace while protecting our kids or neglecting ourselves. This behavior pops up its ugly head when you least expect it, like the dusty Whac-A-Mole down at the godforsaken Chuck E. Cheese. When we sacrifice who we are or who we are meant to be in order to keep people around or to make someone love us, we slowly chip away, bit by bit, at our purpose here on earth. Eventually, what you'll have left is some rough surfaces and jagged edges that require a whole lot of superglue or require you to sand them down and make them fit back together.

As you grow up and learn to find your own way, all of those childhood influences and situations matter. But eventually, you find your own words and truly figure out how you feel about things and learn how to stand up for yourself. You realize that we all have a mixed bag of stories, family expectations, and habits. We can't blame everything on our childhood, can we? Because my childhood was pretty normal.

"Normal."

What is that, anyway?

2

LIVING ON LIKES

"Hey, girl! I would love to get together with you next time you are in town. I have just started selling (fill in the blank), and I just know you would LOVE these products! I would LOVE to send you some samples and see if you like them. Would you do me a favor and go like my page and tag 5 friends who might enjoy this amazing opportunity, too? I appreciate any push you may be able to offer my team. Also, I am making more money now staying home with my kids and thought you might like this opportunity to create the flexibility for the life of your dreams. You would be a great member of our team. Think about it!"

Look here, Morgan, I have not heard from you since 1992. But yeah, I will look you up next time I am in town. I am sure we have a lot in common these days. Let's don't pretend you and I are something that we're not. What you are really saying is, "Hey, girl. I need you to drink my Kool-Aid and start an auto draft each month out of your bank account!" Can I just Venmo you twenty dollars and call it a day? Will that work for you, Morgan?

I would rather ride on the back of an overflowing garbage truck on a steamy August day in the South than ride on that multilevel networking train.

If you are part of a multilevel marketing network, I wish you all the best. I wish you nothing but success and prosperity with that thing that you feel is best for your family. I just wish you would stop messaging me.

I think the biggest oxymoron on the World Wide Web right now is a "twenty-one-year-old life coach." Are you kidding me right now?

Oh, you have a whopping 600 followers and are making a killin' doing this life-coaching gig? Who, may I ask, are your clients? I'll be sure to hire you next time I need to get unstuck with choosing a college major—psychology or mechanical engineering—to keep my parents off my back. Or when I need to learn how to balance my checking account, I will look you up, oh wise life coach. You are the knower of all things at the ripe old age of twenty-one.

I have birthed two giant babies, birthed one giant divorce,

and gathered myself by the bootstraps to make a new life in my forties, but I will be sure to hire the life coach who has successfully launched her business from her fully furnished room in the Chi Omega house. Here, take my $250 and help me find my best self, would ya?

Social media's likes have given us a false sense of security and success. Are we all just dwelling in a false reality now? A Chi Omega who thinks she is changing a world that she has yet to even experience. Or the stay-at-home mom who has tied her soul and identity to a cosmetic brand that is sweeping the globe, yet I see her in the aisle at Walmart with Oil of Olay in her shopping cart.

The whole world has witnessed us all acting like plumb fools for likes. The Tide pod challenge almost killed you people. The Kylie lip challenge gave every young girl in America a big ol' mouth hickey, and the "In My Feelings" challenge was the 2018 version of a Chinese fire drill. Been there, done that. If Kiki has any sense, she will hop over that console and put your pedal to the metal and leave your tail right there in the middle of the road. Then there was the condom challenge. What? Why anyone would want to stick a condom up one nostril, deeply inhale, and then pull it out of the other nostril without trying to gag and puke is beyond me. Yet You-

Tubers were accomplishing exactly that for views and likes. I can't even with you people. Lest we forget the challenge that started them all: the ice bucket challenge. Look here, Brandi, you ain't fooling no one in your little white tank top with the new girls propped up on (cold) display. I'm pretty sure your ice bucket challenge had nothing to do with supporting ALS. Can you tell me exactly how much money you raised to support that medical research? Naw. But you sure had plenty of folks researching your own medical interventions.

When the likes showed up unsolicited on my filter-face video, the whole world (or what felt like the whole world) started commenting on my life. Then Miranda Lambert shared one of my videos, and I died a thousand deaths. The likes spiked, and in an instant I had more likes than I knew what to do with. The likes came pouring in. Each morning and each night, thousands more. The likes sparked the demand for T-shirts and coffee mugs and shows. A new reality was presented to me within weeks. I was living in a new reality. People were liking this stuff. People were liking . . . me?

Shortly thereafter, the dislikes started rolling in. Except there is no thumbs-down for disliking something on social media. So the dislikes come with words and emojis. It didn't take long for me to realize that this is serious soul-searching business. Every day. Putting myself out there online for public review. Thank goodness my skin grew thick in my childhood, mostly from snow cones, but I learned early on that a stranger's negative words have no power over me. I learned to give it no power. Call it out. Bury it and move on.

But now I *am* in the business of entertainment, living on likes. Except the difference is I know that the likes are not life at all. They are moments in time. Nods. A nod here and a nod there. Those nods may buy tickets to one of my shows, or they may not. Those nods may share one of my videos, or they may not.

My favorite kinds of likes are the ones that go the extra mile and come to my in-box. Like the one from a shirtless man with an '80s mustache. He refers to me as "hot babe." Every sentence has "hot babe" in it. "Hey hot babe. I miss you hot babe. Can't wait to talk to you hot babe." OK, eww. Put a shirt on for your next profile picture, man. I am not going to entertain this nonsense, but he persists, and the messages keep on coming. So do his nipples.

Then there are the messages that come to my in-box with heart-wrenching stories of overcoming adversity and illness. Those likes come with purpose, and I am forever changed by them. Messages that encourage me to keep on making people laugh and give a bright spot to an otherwise dark day. The pinnacle of the likes is when I get to meet one of those in-box stories in person at a show. The likes show up in the flesh. Except for the shirtless man—my whole team knows to be on the lookout for that joker. It is a complete circle that makes me realize that the little thumbs-up button comes with a story each and every time. The thumbs-up from complete and total strangers make this work meaningful. Not my stories from the ob-gyn or the checkout line at Walmart. It's the followers' stories. The stories of cancer, depression, grief, addiction, sacrifice, and redemption. Those are the stories that deserve the likes. All of them.

Last Christmas, my thirteen-year-old daughter asked for a lighting kit so she could start posting makeup and skin-care tutorials on Instagram and YouTube. STOP THE MUSIC. I mean, who doesn't love a twenty-five-minute dissertation from a young girl who has just contoured her face, with what can only be compared to pancake batter, to create cheekbones while breathing heavily into the microphone. This is all that I could envision would happen when she made her Christmas request.

As her mom, of course, I was proud of her entrepreneurial spirit and her desire to invest in her own interests. As her mom, I was also scared to death for her self-esteem. She is a spirited young lady who has never shied away from attention. But I worried about the likes. She has been protected from public school, where kids learn to sink or swim. She has been somewhat sheltered from those pressures and allowed to grow up closely snuggled against Mama Bear's chest. Thirteen is a soft, fragile place, where the desire for belonging is raging out of control. My job as her mom (and her dad's job) is to serve as her compass. Helping her find her North Star—which direction she is to travel to know who she is and whose she is. My job is to help her stand firm on a foundation that is built from feelings of safety, security, and belonging. Her Instagram tutorials were short-lived, but I foresee them resurfacing in the future in some capacity. Perhaps it's the criticisms in adolescence that give us the chance to teach our children what's out there doing harm.

My hero, Brené Brown, says in her book *Braving the Wilderness* (and I believe social media is some folks' wilderness): "Stop walking through the world looking for confirmation that you don't belong. You will always find it because you've made that your mission. Stop scouring people's faces for evidence that you're not enough. You will always find it because you've made that your goal. True belonging and self-worth are not goods; we don't negotiate their value with the world."

When I was going through my divorce, I found myself searching and scouring social media for things that had the potential to hurt me. I was like a homeless person rummaging through the trash every day, not for survival, just rifling through trash for any trace of evidence. Clicking on anyone's profile who might have something negative to say about me to my soon-to-be ex. I was looking for pictures that didn't include me. I was looking for clues of how he would attempt to live life without me. I was looking for our friends who might choose to walk with him through the divorce instead of with me. I was looking for ways he might blame me. I was looking for a perception he might try to paint of me. I was creating false stories and scenarios in my head and determined to make myself a victim. I WAS NOT A VICTIM. I WAS A VICTOR. I had fled with my two children and found us a place of peace where our family could heal and thrive. I WAS A CONQUEROR. Yet I continued to search through the trash day in and day out. I was unknowingly searching for something that would hurt me, until a friend said these words to me:

"Heather, what are you going to do if you find what you are looking for? Are you going to confront him and make yourself look absolutely ridiculous? No.

"If you find something that upsets you, does this change your course of action? No.

"If he says just the right thing online, publicly for strangers to read, is this going to salvage your marriage? No.

"The only person being hurt by this searching is YOU. The only person suffering here is YOU. The only person who can unfollow and change what you see and have access to every day is YOU. It is hurting no one but you. So get yourself together and start unfollowing these common denominators. You can friend them again in a few years when the anger has cooled off. And who the heck cares if they know you unfriended or unfollowed them; you aren't around to hear them talk about you. Most people do not have the courage to say to your face what they say behind your back. So for now, CLICK THE BUTTON, HEATHER."

This is exactly what Brené Brown meant in her book: "We don't negotiate our value with the world. The truth about who we are lives in our hearts. Our call to courage is to protect our wild heart against constant evaluation." I was looking for someone to tell me I didn't belong. I was looking for someone to hurl insults at me. I was looking for the snarling, good ol' New Testament gnashing of teeth and casting out of demons. I was looking for judgment because I thought I deserved it. I was looking for my own identity since mine was unsafely placed in a marriage at a young age. Lo and behold, marriage turned out *not* to be the foundation on which someone's identity should be built. (That's a topic for a whole separate book, but I hope you all can incorporate that into your Sunday-school lesson this week for all the young girls to hear.)

Powerful clicking, unliking, and unfollowing. What freedom it gives. But please, don't announce to the world that you are cleaning out your online friends. Walk in maturity. This is not for show. This is for you. This is your power. Don't hand it back over to their opinions. I love the "I am taking time off from Facebook" announcement that plants seeds in others' minds. *Oooh, maybe something happened, or maybe she is wise beyond her years. I wish I had her strength.* NO! Stop all of that. Go in peace. Go in silence.

The beauty of the social-media world is this simple fact: WE HOLD THE POWER IN OUR HANDS. We have the power to decide whom we follow and what we follow. (Except Siri. She is clearly in cahoots with the Home Depot and listens for you to mention a new barbecue grill, and then all of a sudden, those ads from the Home Depot's Fourth of July sale show up in your news feed—I am not talking about that. *Hey, Siri, why don't you mind your own business, mkay?*)

I took back the power I had given to so many people for too long. Their posts were interrupting my workday, interrupting my recovery, and eventually would interrupt my reconciliation. When you can take a step back and identify the behaviors (online or not) that keep you in a place of pain, that is the first step on the road to freedom. Recognize it and move on. You can take back your power. If I can, you can.

Perhaps it was those moments that prepared me for this career as a comedienne. I have the ability to overlook the negative trolls online who pounce on my material when it posts. I have the ability to give the right kind of power and emotion to the likes. I know their place, and I know their role in this online dance that we do.

People like me for how I make them feel when they watch the videos. People don't like ME. They barely know me. Women like me because I give them a reason for a girls' night out to come to a show with their girlfriends. The husband likes me because he likes hearing his wife laugh for the first time since she lost her mother, so he buys her tickets to a show. The truth is, what you are liking isn't me; it's what you know of me. It's my sarcasm that you like. You like my ability to say what you are thinking about the folks who post about their CrossFit workouts or the things you want to say to the crazy baseball moms.

You might not even recognize average ol' me in the grocery store if you saw me. Yes, I still have to go to the grocery store and do laundry and pick up my kids. The likes didn't change any of that. The likes didn't change my joy or happiness.

I once read some very wise advice from Mark Cuban, the *Shark Tank* billionaire who owns the Dallas Mavericks. It was 2016, the Powerball lottery had reached an all-time high of $1.6 billion, and America was going crazy. Everyone was talking about it. Your hairdresser, the grocery-store clerk, the preacher, your grandma . . . everyone.

Cuban was interviewed and offered up his advice to the soon-to-be billionaire; he said, "If you weren't happy yesterday, you won't be happy tomorrow. If you were happy yesterday, you are going to be a lot happier tomorrow."

I know that I hit the like jackpot in 2017 and the years following—it was the right post at the right time (woulda been nice to hit that $1.6 billion, though). The likes that drive my business do not drive my happiness. They are simply a marker that I am doing something right. If you asked my children how many people like their mother's Facebook page, they'd have no clue. I have no clue. My parents have no clue. Ask my manager, because she is the only one who definitely has a clue! Waking up with hundreds of thousands of likes on my Facebook page didn't change me. The likes didn't make me someone I am not (a sarcastic Southern sweetheart—wink). The likes just changed my path. They just changed the trajectory of my career and the way I will provide for my children. Our belonging is not up for negotiation based on how many followers we have. Our value is not determined by the comments section. Our value comes from deep within.

Here's a story from an unknown source:

There is a legend that the ancient gods were discussing where to hide the secret of peace and joy. They did not want humanity to find it before they could appreciate it. They had a great debate about where they could hide it. One of the gods suggested, "We should hide it at the peak of the highest mountain." After some discussion, it was determined that it would be found too fast. They also discussed the deepest forest, the deepest sea, and the hottest desert, all with the same conclusion. Then the wisest god stood up and proclaimed that he knew where to hide it. He spoke slowly and calmly. "Hide it in the human heart. That is the last place they will look."

3

SPOKEN LIKE A
TRUE MILLENNIAL

The English language is in a crisis—a real American crisis. Blame it on the Kardashians or the men in skinny jeans, but I am not sure I can keep up with all of this new vernacular. We like to act like this is a new thing. It's not. In the '50s and '60s, everything was "groovy." My generation said things like "gag me with a spoon" and "your mama," but for some reason no one says that anymore. *As if.* (*Shape of an L on my forehead.*)

When a twentysomething literally says the words "literally" and "like," like, forty-seven times in literally one sentence, like, my face literally begins to flush, my palms literally get sweaty, and, like, I literally can't hear anymore because my ears are bleeding. Like, I literally stop listening, but they keep on literally talking.

Hey, girl, I literally am not hiring you. Get out of my office. Like, literally.

Just last week, my babysitter said "IDK" in normal conversation. She said I-D-K.

(*Crickets.*) (*Looking around.*)

At first, I thought she was spelling a bad word like I used to do when my children were toddlers. C-R-A-P. Or maybe she was describing a DKNY handbag and just messed it up. Nope. She used "IDK" as a real word in a real sentence. For those of you who have no idea what she intended, she meant "I don't know."

CMC (call me crazy), but all these new words have me wondering how to crack the code on today's streets. Am I now the corny ('90s term) mom who embarrasses her son by trying to be cool with today's language? No matter how cool I really am, he will never let me get away with upgrading my vocabulary. I do, however, have something to say that translates seamlessly every single time: *Clean your room, or you are grounded.* Now THAT is one phrase that spans the generations and has withstood the test of time.

I digress.

I would now like to pause for a brief moment to acknowledge the most brilliant millennial word I know: "bougie."

bou·gie /ˈbooZHē/

adjective

Aspiring to be a higher class than one is. Derived from bourgeois—meaning middle/upper class, traditionally despised by communists.

COMMUNISTS?

If you are wearing a Walmart wind suit (also a '90s term) while carrying a giant Louis Vuitton on your shoulder, you are despised by everyone including the communists. And until now, we didn't have a word for people like you, but thanks to millennial jargon, we have been set free!

The struggle is real, I get it. It's hard to say all the proper words. So many words and modifiers. Why be so basic and speak real English? No need. As long as you stay woke, you won't have to communicate with any other generation if you can help it.

My generation is actually to blame for creating this nonsense, because we gifted the world with texting and social media. Millennials have grown up with shorthand. Their language has developed from their predominantly text-based communication and was kinda developed out of necessity. So whether we know what "on fleek" or "lit" means, we'd better get with the program. Look, I am not asking y'all to talk as country as me. I am just asking you to stop making up words that don't mean anything to people over the age of forty. You can't just go around deciding which words deserve an abbreviation and which don't. Some old man down at the dictionary headquarters gets to decide that for the rest of the world.

When my ex-husband started dating a twenty-three-year-old, my first question was "What do they possibly have to talk about? What do they have in common? They don't even speak the same language." I was mortified at the thought of my ex trying to act cool because #thestruggleisreal to be cool enough with people our own age, much less someone who is barely out of college. A man in his forties marries a young trophy wife with whom he has nothing in common. What on earth. Maybe he had mastered the new words. Maybe his dating goals were indeed Netflix and chill. I don't know.

I was very judgmental and a little condescending, I admit it. I never imagined in a million years that my children would have a twentysomething big sister. Um, I mean stepmom. So cliché, but it fits. And so does she. She fits. She loves my children, and I love her, and she loves me. She's more than we could've ever asked for, and that's what counts. Totes.

There are a few things that millennials have gotten right, though.

Millennials are the only generation that knows how to revert a pdf to a Word document, and I'm not mad about it. Talk about them all you want to Mr. CEO, but you know as well as I do that when you need tech help, you are hollering for twenty-seven-year-old Skylar down the hall. You can't stand his skinny ties, but you need him stat.

I am a little low-key jelly of the relaxed professional spirit they possess. I, too, prefer to show up when I get around to it and cut out early because of my caffeine needs. When I lived in Colorado, there was nothing quite like sipping coffee on my sofa while looking at a snowcapped Pikes Peak. That was where my finest inspiration and work happened. If I had to wear a suit and sit in a cubicle all day, I would die a thousand deaths. Can I just work in yoga pants and oversized plaid shirts? What is wrong with that? See, I may be a Gen Xer, but I am picking up what y'all are putting down.

They are coffee snobs and sushi connoisseurs; they love charcuterie boards, and they know craft beer. But the way they talk is next-world stuff.

Millennials have made things popular that other generations have been doing for ages. Like skipping breakfast and calling it intermittent fasting. BRILLIANT! My generation called that an eating disorder and sent your tail to counseling. Millennials took the 1980s man with a mustache, beard, polyester pants, and gold-rimmed glasses, lost the dad bod and added tattoos, and then called him a hipster. My generation called him Mike, the used-car salesman.

You know what else millennials have changed? Weddings. A WHOLE PARADIGM SHIFT!

No more church aisles, no more standard old hymns, no more pimento cheese sandwiches at the Fellowship Hall reception. Heck no. They have taken it to a whole new level—to old shipping warehouses and barns with rent-by-the-hour pastors who have super-duper grizzly beards and wear leather suspenders with their jeans to preside over the vows. They have receptions under canopies with string lights and lanterns. They don't serve cake, nuts, and butter mints anymore. They have photo booths, donut walls, self-serve candy bars, and cupcake towers. And you better BYOS (bring your own straw) because these jokers are in the business of saving the sea turtles at this wedding, too.

Millennials even use their entrepreneurial spirit to crowdfund their honeymoons to exotic bucket-list places like Fiji or New Zealand. As far as I am concerned, that's the best use of that degree in entrepreneurship that your parents paid for. You want to know where my generation went to honeymoon?

Pigeon Forge.

That's because all of our grannies were paying for it. Granny didn't crowdfund. She didn't ask for money on Kickstarter. She got that cash right out of the rusty Altoids can she keeps tucked in the Naturalizer shoebox hidden deep in her closet. We didn't care about exotic destinations, because we had to wait seven to ten days to get our film processed, and by that time, your friends and family didn't care about your pictures or selfies. There was no posting midair pics jumping off a pier into crystal blue water. There were no feet-in-the-sand pics to post from the other side of the globe. We took a pic at the top of a Ferris wheel at Dollywood. THAT WAS ROMANCE. That was the beginning of a long, cheap life together.

Before millennial weddings took over, our humble lives began with the money collected during the first dance—the "Money Dance." This was where your friends and family pinned dollar bills to your dress or tuxedo while you were dancing at the reception. You asked your third cousin twice removed, who has a knack for flower arranging, to "do" your flowers. But that's all we could afford. The rest was fake ferns and ficus trees you could borrow.

Millennials have made such an impact on our society that they have warranted their own Monopoly game. Instead of buying property, you buy experiences and trade hot destinations. You end up living in your parents' basement or on a friend's couch. You can buy stock in the thrift shop or the farmers' market. The tagline on the box reads: "Forget real estate. You can't afford it anyway." I may not be part of this generation, but this game sounds a little more realistic to me. Well played Hasbro, well played.

A millennial's schedule is always negotiable. They aren't locked into efficiency and productivity. Unless they are downloading a mobile update—then their time is the most valuable thing on the planet. That technology had better work in a millisecond or they are losing their cotton-picking mind. Pop that anxiety medicine and calm down, would you? And millennial babysitters are THE WORST. On the day before, they confirm with all the sweet words: "Can't wait to see you guys. She is the most adorable baby ever. (*Emoji Emoji Emoji*)." Thirty minutes before: "I am so sorry. I have to cram for my final tomorrow and I didn't get any sleep last night and I also have to walk my neighbor's dog, so I don't think I can babysit tonight." An hour later, she is spotted posing on Instagram with her burrito bowl and two friends.

I can't with you.

This is the generation that has grown up with living life publicly. But I think they forget that we "real people" can see them and hear them. We read their rants about the barista getting their order wrong and how their whole day is ruined because of it. First of all, my grandparents would roll over in their graves to know we are spending five dollars on one cup of coffee. Second of all, if your barista has the power to "literally ruin your life," then your barista is a very, very powerful person. I would like to meet them.

Not all millennials deserve such a bad rep, though. They are the generation most likely to donate their time or work for a cause. They have good hearts. They are skeptical and use their skepticism to challenge politicians, faith leaders, and government policy. They are focused on experiences, less on acquiring material possessions to fulfill the American dream, and, in fact, they have really reshaped that American dream as we know it. They are reducing the divorce rate because they simply aren't getting married. And if you're not married, you can't get divorced, right? Sounds like a good solution to a bad problem that my generation couldn't solve.

When I need some creative energy, guess who I want in my circle? Yep, you guessed it. The guy in skinny jeans and a man bun. When I need someone to produce something with technology, who do I call? It sure ain't Ghostbusters. Millennials know how to travel, and they aren't afraid to. Travel will always be a part of their future. They have grown up with Airbnb and Uber. They know how to get around and get what they want. They aren't intimidated by traveling to places unknown. They care as much about mental health as they do about physical health. They care about eating right and living right. They would rather have a few good friends than please everyone they meet. They aren't really into impressing people. They really aren't interested in fitting into the box. They are into intentional living.

Millennials push us to know why we are doing the things we do and who we really are. They really can push us to be better people if we let them. They bring a whole new energy to our lives and help us recenter our priorities. If we can get past the language barrier, we might just learn a thing or two about ourselves. If we can get past the age gap, we may just fall in love with millennials. They are generous and kind and good-hearted.

I know because I am dating one.

4

YO-YO SKILLS

It's a math problem as old as time. If I eat three pounds of chocolate cake today, how does it become ten pounds on my body tomorrow? There has to be a biology class that I missed somewhere along the way. You know, I was a Bible college dropout, so maybe that's where I was supposed to learn that lesson. Oh, wait, we didn't learn science there, only creation.

Do you want to know how long it takes to lose eighty pounds of baby weight? I would like to know, too! I have been whittling away at these stubborn last few pounds since 2006, when my second child was born. And gosh, I am tired of whittling. My hands are stiff, my knife needs sharpening, and my spine is tired of being hunched over. I am about one diet away from trying crack. You?

When we were kids in the '80s and '90s, we learned about food in a pyramid. Eat a lot of the good stuff but only a little of that triangle at the top—the candy, soda, cake. Perhaps that food pyramid was all wrong, because I have been hanging out here at the bottom with all the bread and pasta, thinking that I am a real winner—me and Oprah. Then the jeans don't fit, and I am back to black coffee and MiraLAX.

Now they say that the whole food pyramid is wrong. A whole generation of people are left out here wandering the grocery aisles. In 2020, I am so confused. I don't know if milk is good for us or if it's going to rot my intestines. Am I supposed to be fermenting my own kombucha now? My family comes from a long line of bootleggers, so the fermenting work should come natural to me. Wheat or no? Is fake sugar going to kill me? Should I just go straight juice all the time even if I start losing my hair? What about eggs, yay or nay? We all know guac is "good" fat, but too much gives you gout. Eat grapefruit for breakfast, drink cold water when you first wake up, shoot apple cider vinegar. Someone just please wake me up when potatoes make a comeback. For the love. No wonder we are all fat. We are just trying to keep up. We are just trying to get food on the table to feed our babies and bellies.

One thing that has changed since we were kids is the amount of food choices we have. Good Lord above. When I was growing up, there was one fast-food joint, and it came with a playground so that you burned calories while you ate. Or you would get salmonella from the ball pit, and that would help you keep your weight in check. There were no super-size options. There were no double burgers with bacon. My mom wouldn't even let me get fries. Just a burger. Why do you think I snuck bologna sandwiches at midnight? Now we have 7,437,983 types of chips in the supermarket and any type of cuisine you want, ridden with salt and butter, delivered to your front door. *Look, I haven't cooked a thing in eight months, and I may never have to cook again. Praises.*

Now Amazon is delivering food with drones. Next, I will be able to hire a tall, handsome man named Enrique to bring me dinner and feed it to me and tell me I am pretty while I lie on the couch. Can this please be my new reality? We can get what we want, how we want it, and when we want it. Totally healthy. Can I get chips and queso delivered at midnight when I'm already changed into my pajamas? Is late queso delivery a thing? If not, it totally should be. My friend lives in a college town that has a cookie delivery company that delivers warm cookies until three A.M. Look, I know that delivery service is catering to college kids who are staying up late cramming for finals, but I am a tired mom who binge-watches *Sister Wives* late at night like I am going to be tested on it. *Just leave the queso on the doorstep and move along, delivery boy. Nothing to see here.*

Oh, yeah, I am a pro at this yo-yo dieting thing. *Oh, it's not a diet? Thanks, Marie Osmond. It's a lifestyle change.* I get it, I've used that line before, too. I have read all the books and blogs, and seen all the infomercials. All it takes is one birthday dinner or girls' night out to fall off and be totally under that wagon. I like to think that I am self-sacrifical—laying down my life (diet) for my community. Taking one for the team. Diet always starts again on Monday. Wash, rinse, repeat.

And repeat again. I am pretty sure my body is two parts Diet Coke, one part hot fudge sundae. I can go up and down on a scale so fast that it makes Usain Bolt jealous.

I once heard that there are two types of eaters: those who restrict and those who permit. I am a restricter. Kinda like my religious upbringing. We find the rules, lists, and calorie counting to be liberating. If I don't see it or smell it, if I don't buy it or keep it in the house, it won't hurt me. So I restrict it all—everything. I can't enjoy any good food because my body will betray me and I will surely gain weight with one whiff of that cereal aisle, so I will have none of it. I won't even look in its direction. I will not even drive near the local Krispy Kreme, because I will be tempted. OK, yes, I will. I will do a U-turn in the middle of a seven-lane freeway when that "Hot Now" sign is blinking. It's like a moth to a flame. It's like an addict on Ambien. It's like the red-light district blinking its lustful ways in my direction. That hot, soft donut is the bane of my existence and the bane of my bathing suit. And the reason I made it through the summer without putting on a bathing suit.

To us restricters, diet is the name of the game.

DIET = Did I Eat That?

DIET = Do I Eat Today?

DIET = Don't Indulge Every Time

Every Monday we start one. I will not go to that birthday party because . . . cake. What's that you say? Celery juice will rid me of all my body's transgressions and launch my metabolism into outer space? Grab my helmet. Cabbage soup is the weight-loss secret of the stars? Mmmmm, gas . . . count me in. I will consume nothing but. Only eating one meal a day at 2:30 P.M. will change my life? Done. Setting my clock now. Tell me what I need to cut out, and I will do it now. Give me rules. Give me a chart. Give me a five-gallon drum of apple cider vinegar and a straw. Give me vials that I have to pee in to measure ketosis. Restriction works. It's like holding that raging bull in a pen at the rodeo. We know that if and when the gate opens, the wild energy is out, and the beast is holding back nothing. That is what happens when I pass a Chick-fil-A, and then, well, you know the rest. The sauce. The frozen lemonade. Diet starts again on Monday.

Atkins, Weight Watchers, Paleo, keto, vegan, South Beach. I've done Whole30, and it only took a whole thirty minutes before I realized I wasn't going to chop all those fruits and vegetables required. I even made up my own "Heather Land Diet":

Breakfast: Black coffee and one egg
Midmorning: Diet Coke
Lunch: Sliced turkey and celery, Diet Coke
Afternoon snack: Coffee
Dinner: 483 slices of pizza

I have gone from counting fat grams to counting carbs to counting steps. What I really need to be counting is sheep—the only way to keep it off is just to stay asleep.

I am never satisfied with this ol' body of mine, always needing to lose. Always. It is exhausting. But yet . . . still not willing to go to the gym. I have boundaries, people. I can't do it all. I went to Zumba once, and all that Latin music had me craving enchiladas before I was outta there. So I restrict the exercise, too. No need to try to be all things.

And yet I agree with Julia Child: people who love to eat are typically the best people. Standing around a kitchen with a glass of wine and a charcuterie board is my favorite pastime. It is where we share life. In the kitchen. It's the heart of all of our homes. When a new home is built, the kitchen is the most important room in the house. When we share a meal, we enter into community with one another. Inviting someone over to your home for a meal is a genuine invitation to share life. Over a plate of food is where we get to know one another. Sharing a meal is how we show we care to those who are hurting or in need. Setting aside time for a meal, around a table without distractions, is a genuine way to live and love your people. Sharing a meal is the most intimate act you can participate in with your clothes on. Relationships begin when you share a dish together. It's why potlucks and dinners on the ground endure; it's why an apron is a sex symbol, why two people serving themselves out of the same carton of Chinese counts as togetherness and ordering one dessert with two spoons feels like romance.

We grieve, we eat. We celebrate, we eat. We work too much, we eat. We are lonely, we eat. We are happy, we eat. Food is tied to so many emotional things for us. It is our drug of choice. It satisfies for the moment. It feels good. It can become a companion when we are lonely. And it is not just for us Southern folks who grew up believing that hash-brown casserole is a vegetable. Food is the cultural norm for celebration and sadness all around the globe.

But now our daughters are learning how to read food labels and order sugar-free macchiatos. Our daughters first hear the word "fat" coming out of our mouths to describe our own bodies. They don't have a fighting chance in this mean ol' world. And then we all dread the day our daughters come home from school with hurt feelings because someone made fun of them for their appearance. Yet they have heard us criticize and diet and critique in our own home. Now they hear it from someone on the playground, and it begins to take root in their view of themselves. They start to believe this is the normal way to view their bodies.

In sixth-grade math class, the boy behind me leaned over and whispered, "You're so fat you could roll over a dollar and make four quarters." Thirty-two years later, I still remember like it was yesterday. I've never felt beautiful enough. I've never felt skinny enough, as if skinny is the metric. If someone called me a liar it wouldn't affect me, because I know that is not who I am. But call me fat, and you have just attacked my value. Why? Because as women our value is tied to our appearance. Sticks and stones may break my bones. But tell me I am fluffy, and I will surely die.

It is all around us, the pressure to look good. The pressure to match the competition. The pressure to satisfy a standard. The unattainable. And if striving to look a certain way isn't the particular thorn in your side, perhaps that next WOD goal or the next Ultra Marathon is. (*Eye roll.*)

We have tied our souls to shame and guilt that have us trapped, not food. It was never the food's fault. So we binge and purge in different ways. There are times I have been at my thinnest but still felt like the fattest woman in the room. And that, my friends, has NOTHING to do with the scale. That kind of perception comes from the inside. From the deepest guts of my identity and value and worth.

We always blame the media for bombarding our minds with unrealistic images and photoshopped bodies. But I dare say that this is a self-perpetuating problem within our gender and within our homes. Moms casting their own insecurity and weight-loss burdens onto their children without knowing it. Speaking words of shame when Mom sees herself in a picture. Those little ears are listening. Those little perceptions are being shaped about their purpose. Shaming a young boy for wanting another bag of cookies when his body is growing so fast that he burns 9 million calories in a day. He could eat the entire pantry and still be hungry. We are telling little girls how pretty they are and never complimenting a little girl on the five-hundred-piece puzzle she just completed or the second-grade science fair she just won. We have made a woman's entire existence and purpose about the way she looks. And if the world tells us we look good, then that must mean the world has taken notice of us. We have been seen.

The truth is, I can only name about five women in my life who have a healthy relationship with food and their bodies. I have thin friends who are obsessed with losing weight, living their life as if "I have to look this way or no one will love me." Body image is no respecter of persons.

It's all the same. We are all in the same sinking shame boat. *My only role here is to be pretty and lovely. Without an acceptable physical appearance I have nothing to offer, and I am nothing of value.* I am pretty sure this is NOT what our mother's generation had in mind when they burned their bras. We have to change the narrative on this. For the sake of our daughters and granddaughters and great-granddaughters. And for our sons and grandsons and great-grandsons.

We have to stop our friends when they shame themselves before they take the first bite. We have to stop the shaming in the dressing room, dead in its tracks. We have to stop the thoughts before the words are formed about our own appearance. We have to stop the cellulite shaming at the pool. Stop it. I will hear none of it. And I hope you will shut down my shaming, too.

Perhaps the weight we need to lose isn't on our body. Fact. The weight we need to lose is the fear of being unlovable. The fear of loneliness. The fear of abandonment. The weight of broken relationships and the impasse of unforgiveness. The weight of a wound that you have hidden away in your junk drawer. The weight of dreams gone unfulfilled. The weight of the voice inside you that is dying to be heard. The weight of everyone else's problems that you have carried for too long.

Instead of a new fad diet, what if we started the right kind of diet?

DIET = Determined, Intentional, Encouraging, Trail-
   blazing
DIET = Disciplined, Intelligent, Empowered, Truthful
DIET = Deliberate, Insightful, Extraordinary, Trans-
   parent

For once, let's focus on fattening up our values. Chew on some good meat. Restrict the bad, and only consume the good. "Trim the fat" of the unnecessary stuff. Let's focus on restricting the things that are really hurting us. Imagine the damage done by the carbohydrates of toxic people in our lives. A warm loaf of homemade bread covered in butter. Those carbs seem fluffy and good at first but just leave you feeling fluffy and bad the day after. They are deceivingly tasty but filled with hidden junk that brings you down. If we could just get rid of the bread, then we would slim right up. Count all the calories in your unhealed wounds. Sure the higher the calories, the better it tastes, but the bigger the wound, the more it takes to burn off. What about the fat grams in the shame you're toting around? That shame buries itself deep in your veins, and you sometimes forget it's there. If your heart is the sum of all the trans-fat you've eaten, one day it will show the signs of wear and tear of shame—the invisible killer.

The widow maker. Maybe we all need a new body-mass-index number after shedding the mom guilt? Pressure to measure up to Pinterest's definition of a good mom. I don't know about you, but that pressure is accomplishing nothing in my home, just making a bunch of women cray.

If we eat for any reason other than hunger, food will not be what satisfies us. Should I get an infomercial going on this? I just high-fived myself for a nugget of truth. Weight loss is not the key to weight loss. Loving ourselves is. Being present in our bodies and spirits, being fully alive, informs us of what to eat and when. When we value ourselves more than the guy sitting behind us in math class, we can believe in ourselves. When we stop struggling, hiding, faking, manipulating, and controlling, we learn to be OK in our own skin. We have to reteach ourselves about our loveliness. We have to retrain our minds and hearts to handle our bodies with grace. When the shape of your body no longer shapes your existence, the weight will disappear—physically and emotionally.

I think the key to weight loss isn't a diet at all. It doesn't look like restriction. It looks like generosity and mercy. I dare say this might be your (our) most important work. It requires humility, honesty, and a teachable spirit. If you need help with this, get help. If you need medical intervention, it is 2020—go get it. If you need a friend on this journey, find one who can speak wisdom to you.

Give yourself room to love yourself, not punish. I want this, don't you? It's a daily decision, and I am not there yet. I know that I am not where I used to be, but every day I make strides to show up and see my body, my weight, and my health as a gift. I hope you can, too.

5

PARENT TRAP

I thought raising teenagers would be like an episode of *That '70s Show*—groovy kids chilling in the basement, trying to navigate acne, dating, and getting their driver's licenses. I thought I would be the corny parent who popped in every once in a while to ask the right questions and sometime state a good lesson. My kids would come to me with their problems and look to all my wisdom and experience with respect and adoration. They would want to hang out with me because . . . tattoos. I am the cool mom, remember?

I would like to suggest that raising teenagers is more like an episode of *Law & Order*, except there is no law or order in the day-to-day interactions in my home anymore. The plots revolve around moral, ethical, or personal dilemmas, and all parties' lives hang in the balance. Mommy's life hangs out in her bedroom screaming into a pillow.

Raising a hormonal teenager is like folding a fitted sheet. No one really knows how to do it, and shoving it in the closet is the only possible solution. It was just a few years ago that my children thought I hung the moon. My daughter wanted to be me, and my son just wanted to be near me. ALL. THE. TIME. Now they criticize my every move and apparently can't make complete sentences when I ask them a question. The eye rolls are so big I can hear them. Can I just tag out for a few years and wait until they show up for that first Thanksgiving of their first year of college? They will appreciate me then, surely. The baby stage was the most exhausting, but the teenage years are the most frustrating. I have a serious case of FOMO: fear of mothering out. I have no more mothering to give.

I wish I had a dime for every book and article I read to prepare for the arrival of a baby so I could afford to buy the bigger book about raising freakin' teenagers. *On Becoming Babywise* and *What to Expect When You're Expecting* did not address this stage. I wish there had been a book called *What to Expect When You Least Expect It*. That would have been more helpful. I loved the baby stage. I was born with a baby doll in my arms. Every childhood picture of me has a baby doll in it. Give me all the babies to hold. Give me all the diapers and burp cloths. I loved it all so much and would do it over a million times. If I wouldn't gain eighty pounds or grow a new set of hemorrhoids, I would volunteer to be a surrogate. But then they grow up. Oh, sure, I can still tell you the proper breastfeeding techniques that helped my babies to latch on every time, but right about now, all I can think about is how to get them to unlatch and get a job. Mommy's done feeding you now.

The pressure of the infant stage was unbearable—all the moms judging themselves, judging others, and offering unsolicited advice—now all of our kids live on Cheetos and Kool-Aid. We are all on a level playing field. *Look here, Lisa, if you have told me once, you have told me a million times about breastfeeding your twins until they were two. We applaud you. We really do. You have hung your hat on that accomplishment, but let's move on, sister, we are all just trying to keep them out of jail now. It takes a village, not your breast milk.*

Something happens when you become a mom that no one tells you about. Once that baby leaves your body, a whole new personality takes over. That personality is ridden with fear that it has never known. Before children, I used to look at older women and wonder when they stopped having fun and when they became so overbearing. Then I became a mom. My brain no longer whipped out information on the fly; it became slug-gish like a computer that hasn't been updated in a while. You start saying things like "Be careful" ALL THE TIME, ON REPEAT. You stay two steps ahead of your wobbly toddler who is still learning to walk. You see the sharp corner on the eye-level glass table long before your child sees it. You become Superwoman and super tired. Keeping them alive is the first part. Giving them a good life is the second part of parenthood that makes us become unrecognizable. We all work so hard to protect them and go to great lengths to give them a good life, "better than the one we had growing up."

It is a trap. It is a comparison trap. Parenthood is a bill of goods that, if we are not careful, we also sell to our children. The parenthood trap can make us believe that life is about all the stuff and all the power we have to provide the stuff. We take our insecurities about our worth as adults and project them onto our children's little lives. We squeeze man-sized problems into adolescent-sized dreams. We live to satisfy our little creatures while we have puke on our shirts and caffeine in our hands. Parents will stop at nothing to help their chil-dren succeed. Parents will do anything to keep their kids on top. Parents will do whatever it takes to give them a leg up. But what happens when our children are no longer the center of our universe? When they are adults? When our children are now the parents? How can they make the switch?

Now, I've already told you I was an only child, but I am not sure you fully understand the magnitude of that statement. I wouldn't necessarily say I was spoiled with material possessions, but I was the center of my parents' universe. If you want to really know someone, all you have to do is ask them about their family's Christmas traditions when they were a kid. Go ahead, do it. That is when all the crazy comes out—family memories knit together by quirky traditions. It's no wonder we all need counseling.

My parents went to such great lengths to convince me that Santa was real that they hired a friend to dress as Santa and come into our home on Christmas Eve. *TAKE THAT, Elf on a Shelf! You have nothing on my parents!* The rent-for-hire Santa was instructed to make enough noise to wake me up, so I could catch him in the flesh by our Christmas tree. And just as they suspected, I found him. Caught him red-handed in our living room. My parents had the best intentions, but those intentions resulted in the adult me believing this was all crap and I was not making my children believe if they didn't want to. Why? Because the emotional damage and embarrassment that believing in Santa well up into the fifth grade caused me is not something I wanted to bestow on my own offspring.

Because I am an only child, I feel a lot of pressure to satisfy my parents' expectations of a family Christmas even though I have my own children now. I fear that if we don't visit their home, they "won't have Christmas."

Last Christmas, the three of us arrived at their home to find my mom busy as a bee in the kitchen. It smelled like a delicious Southern holiday home. Whiffs of chicken pot pie and green bean casserole. Can you smell it now?

"Don't touch that food. It's not for you."

Ummm, excuse me? Whiplash. "Last I checked, I am your child, and you are my mom. There's an unwritten rule somewhere that whenever I am here, regardless of my age, whatever you have is now mine—no questions asked."

Except this day, Glenda was having none of it. There was no sharing, because this food was for Mr. Bill. "His wife told me that this is his favorite recipe."

"Mom, I hate to be the bearer of bad news, but Mr. Bill died two days ago."

But she already knew that, because she makes food for all the deceased folks' families in that little town upon their earthly exit.

My mom was tending to these dishes so gently and tenderly that you would have thought a food critic from *Bon Appetit* magazine was sitting in her dining room. She was wiping the edges, freeing them from crumbs and overflow. She was using her best plates and serving pieces. I stood there in amazement and flat-out jealousy. Can I be dead right now? Can you feed me like you are feeding corpses right now? That Christmas, a dead person's family got all the goods. And there I was acting like a spoiled little child who was going to die of starvation. See, even as adult children, we have roles to play with our parents where we have needs and they are expected to meet them. On time, every time. The parent trap.

We buy presents we can't afford. Decorate the house with so many lights the Griswolds file a complaint to the homeowners association. We all know the lady who has a Christmas tree in every room, Christmas-themed shower curtains, Christmas-themed toilet paper that she hand-stamps with a Christmas stamp and then rolls it back onto the spool. There's one in every bunch. And I am sure her adult kids hate Christmas now. All in the spirit of giving our children a good life. Holidays are just one example.

In the '80s, the tooth fairy was on minimum wage at best. She didn't have much change to spare for snaggletoothed children. That one dollar she left was big money for me. I probably spent it on a *Punky Brewster* poster for my bedroom. These days, moms are expected to account for inflation, and the tooth fairy is running at ten to twenty dollars per tooth. "Hey, at least I am teaching my children about economics," thinks every mom when shoving a twenty-dollar bill under her child's pillow.

Then there are the class parties. Oh, boy. Moms (and dads) hanging out in elementary classrooms like they have never before seen sweet little Mackenzie lick the blue frosting off a cupcake. There's the mom who needs to prove her crafting skills and the mom with the themed goodie bags filled with homemade treats, properly labeled (with a custom monogram) to identify her kid. Kids love class parties, I get it. And some of you parents love them, too. All I am asking is that you sign me up to bring the plates and napkins. And if they have to match the party theme, I am bouncing. Send me a bill.

Take a stroll down to the Little League baseball fields and you will find exhausted parents who spend every weekend and every last cent traveling with their son's competitive baseball team. Hotel rooms, meals, dragging little sister along, all for helping a child pursue a passion. When I was eight, I only had one passion: my Get in Shape Girl tape and my pink Jambox. You hear me?

Prior to my divorce and a few years after, I decided homeschooling was my life's calling. In my mind, homeschooling was a great option for stability and flexibility alike. The kids could be home with me all day. No more running around on someone else's schedule. Life would now be on our time frame. It really gave me a sense of control over one aspect of my otherwise chaotic home. Or maybe it was my attempt to get out of those pesky class party obligations. Yeah, sure, we had class parties during homeschooling. *Hey, kids, let's go eat Mexican for lunch and tell them it's my birthday!* Now I have no idea what grade they are in. I just go by their height and weight. They "look" like they should be in seventh and ninth grade. What used to be "Muffins with Mom" will now be "Mimosas with Mom." What used to be "Donuts with Dad" is now "Do Not Tell Your Dad." I used to drop them off at school with their backpack and a lunch box, and then I started dropping them off at Kroger with a list and my debit card.

I am fortunate to have my children's father participating in this game of parenthood, and even though we are divorced, we are still raising these hoodrats together. We knew that even though our marriage ended, our parenting force did not. We have both brought new love into our lives, and God knows it was for the best, because now the four of us can run a double-down defense. I raise my glass (of prosecco) to all you single ladies grinding through this parenthood trap. You are the real heroes. You need the cape. Heck, you need to be writing all the books. (And if any of you have any teenager advice, throw it my way.)

I have just started this teenage journey and have more years ahead of me than behind me. I have never felt so crazy, so bipolar, in all my life than right now with these teenagers in my home. One day, I am all "You are never ever coming out of your room, mister, you will have no friends, no driver's license, no life everrrrrrr." Two days later: "Here's twenty bucks, take the golf cart and go treat your friends to some ice cream. You don't have to come home, but you can't stay here. Beat it."

I am not totally sure, but I think they can call my bluff now. I am a pushover; they make the rules, I just live here.

What happened to us, people? Where did we go wrong? When I was growing up, we all feared the sound of our daddy's belt flying through the loops of his Levi's. We knew the smackdown was coming if we talked back. We knew we had to be home when the streetlights came on. We knew that our parents were in charge and should be feared. And if you said your mama's name one too many times, she grew horns and shut the place down. They never came to our schools because the principal could also bring the smackdown with his paddle on their behalf—our teachers and principals were just an extension of the enforcers at home. And while I am on the subject, being a teacher has to be the hardest job on the planet. These superhuman individuals give their heart and soul to mastering an academic subject and then spend all the days of their lives raising our rotten children. And if the rotten children aren't bad enough, teachers then have to put up with parents making accusations and criticizing them for giving their kids bad grades and discipline that they deserve. Our children are not the victims of teachers; our children are the victims of jerk parents.

Our parents didn't coddle us during a scuffle with our friends. No, they told us to rub dirt in it and keep going. They were a force to be reckoned with. Now we walk our kids into school, shameless in our *SpongeBob* pajama pants, to protect them from tripping or stubbing their toes. They all have trophies. They all make the team. They won't know hurt if we can help it. Because it hurts us to see them hurt.

When we are supposed to be at our best, the weight of parenthood piles up and takes us down. We take on all the guilt, shame, and judgment of who we think we should be. Do you lock yourself in the bathroom so they won't see you cry tears of insanity and utter exhaustion? I know I have more times than I can count.

I have come to realize that I have only one job in this parenting trap: to show them what love looks like. One goal. Their dad and I did a really bad job of this for many years, but thank God for second chances and third chances and one-thousandth chances. To show them love means to show grace, forgiveness, kindness, respect, and humility. That applies to everyone. Now, let me preach for just a second. If we could see the world through the lens of grace, how much better would we all be? Grace for ourselves and grace to those who may not look like us. Offer forgiveness to people who make mistakes and hurt us. Kindness to strangers and respect for those who have absolutely nothing to offer us in return. And if we can be humble and own the mess, there's nothing that love can't endure.

The truth is, we can't do it all. Moms, are you listening? All the matching outfits and hair bows for family pics, the magazine-worthy home, the French lessons followed by dance classes and the science camps. Kids don't need us to chew out their teachers or referees to ace a class or win a game. Are kids even allowed to flunk a test in school anymore? Kids don't need us at class parties with pumpkin-shaped Rice Krispies Treats. We can't do it all, be at all the things, make all the treats. I would dare say that our kids don't need or even want us to. They want security and safety and warm arms filled with love when they flunk a test or strike out. Kids need us to show them how to navigate this world. Kids need us to help them find their identities and affirm them. Our kids need us to love. They just want love. Love will give our kids confidence. Love will give them security. Love will give them safety. Love will give them joy. Love will give them life.

Just love them.

6

THE HATMAKER

We wear a lot of hats, we ladies. Men, don't stop reading, because you wear a lot of hats, too, but I want to speak to the gals for a minute (because I am one). We are fabulous creatures—bearing children, managing lives and businesses and households. I don't think I could've done life if I hadn't had the encouragement of other women along the way. For whatever season I've seemed to be in, I have always somehow had other women to encourage and help guide me along sanity's narrow path.

Numero uno, the line leader: Granny. This lady has contributed more to my life than potentially every person combined. If I had to list all the things she did for me in the span of her life, we would be here all day, but let me tell you one of the most important. She made me feel accepted. She never judged me, my thoughts, my actions, my motives. She just loved and accepted me always. She made me feel normal. She let me know early on that no matter what I said or did or thought, I was amazing in every way. Well, maybe not EVERY way. She knew I was on the basketball B-team for a reason. But she always made me feel special. She's at the top of the list when it comes to important women in my life.

There have been numerous gals my age along the way who have kept my fire burning as well—accepting the mess that has been me. We all need good friends who can tell us we are killing it in the game of life but who will also tell us when our breath stinks and that we are losing our crap and need to get it together. We need women to tell us when we should stay and when we should go. We need women to hold our hands after the miscarriage or after the diagnosis. We need women to be honest with us when we are in complete denial. We need these kinds of gals in our lives. And I'm lucky, cuz I've got plenty.

Because this is fresh on my brain, let me tell you about the latest woman in my life who's been blazing a trail. She probably doesn't even know about her contribution to my life. We've only known each other for a few short years, but she has been instrumental in leaving a mark on me in this extremely weird season that I've been in. Who is the mystery woman?

Jen Hatmaker.

You don't know her? Let me introduce you. Look her up. You'll find all the information you need and a lot of information that you don't, for that matter. I've been following Jen since I was a little girl. Never mind that she's only a few months older than me. Don't worry about that. She's older, and that's all that matters.

The truth is, I first heard about Jen when I was in the throes of "baby prison," as she calls it. My kids were little, and I needed assistance. She gave it to me in the form of comedic relief via social-media posts and her book *Out of the Spin Cycle*. In those moments, I thought, "Who is this wise one who speaks life to my soul? She knows me. We are friends— she and I. She has been where I am. I feel it. She must be at least seventy-six, but I don't care. We will live out the rest of her days here on earth together until she meets Jesus face to face. She and I—besties for the restie. Never mind that we've never met in real life. She knows . . ."

Clearly, she is not seventy-six, because that would mean I'm seventy-five, and we can all tell that's about fifty-five years from the truth. She is, however, wise beyond her fortysomething years, and she was back then, too—when I was cleaning smeared poop off the walls. When I had two littles, ages five and one, she already had three ahead of me, not to mention the two she and her husband adopted shortly after. She had already gone before me and paved the way. She had written the words that young moms need to hear before they go AWOL. She had learned the secrets to surviving motherhood and was so graciously passing them on to me free of charge (minus the cost of her book). After all, that's what best friends do. She got me through the early years, and I owed her my sanity. Here . . . take my credit card.

Shortly after I was exonerated and freed from my baby prison cell, I discovered there was more to my sidekick than I had previously known. Friends for years now, I am used to her sarcastic, fun-loving personality and her ability to lighten my daily load with laughter, but when she went deep in her book *Interrupted*, she had me wondering if I ever even knew her at all. Not only did she have natural comedic abilities, but she was now showing me a raw, honest look inside her heart and her life of ministry. She was everything I wanted to be. She was my Woman Crush Wednesday. I loved her with my whole heart, and had our paths crossed back then, I was sure she would've loved me, too. I had nothing to offer her but a cold cup of coffee and some laundry to sit on, but she wouldn't have minded. Best friends don't care. Best friends just show up with wine.

Let's fast-forward a few years. Life went on. She raised her growing brood, and I raised mine. She had zero advice to give me regarding my tumultuous marriage, which was a bit of a letdown, but I was glad she and Brandon had their crap together . . . because she was gonna need him in the coming days.

Let it be known, this lady ain't afraid of anybody. She is strong and capable, and when she believes in something, she will stand guns a-blazing. And Jen, in the past few years, has proven it. She has spoken out and stood for our brothers and sisters in the LGBTQ community on many fronts. She has rocked the Christian boat, challenged systems and beliefs, and folks in her circle—in our circle—haven't been too happy about it. Since we hadn't had coffee in a while, I only watched the unfolding from afar. I watched her numbers decline, her books be ripped from shelves, her family be threatened. But why? Because people didn't agree? Because she challenged their mind-sets?

Let me get this "straight" . . . what I'm hearing as I watch this unfold is this: We have to agree to love each other? Is that right? Because if that's the case, Jen and I should've broken up a long time ago. Her long feather earrings are just way too big for my little head, and I cannot adopt those into my life and heart. Actually, I hate them. She also eats chips and guacamole at midnight, and I just can't get on board with that. I must excommunicate her from my life and my library at once.

Look, I understand standing up for beliefs, the same way Jen has done. If you disagree with her, I actually applaud you. Stand up for what you believe in! But I will never understand the hate that comes along with being challenged. "We are Christians, and we don't agree with you, Jen. Therefore, your entire family must suffer and die." WHAT?!? When did this become OK? It has hurt my heart more than anything I could possibly ever disagree with her about. And for the record, about most things . . . I don't.

I don't have all the answers. I'm no theologian. But I am a human, and so is she. Her views, beliefs, and opinions are just that—hers. I don't know all the things she believes in or doesn't. I don't need that in order to be her friend or stand beside her to do the good work of encouraging people. But I do know this: disagreeing with someone doesn't automatically mean they have no value, that their words aren't relevant, and that you can't trust a single thing they say. I do know that. I know that whether you agree or disagree, she is worth your time, your ear—worth your being challenged.

Let's be clear, she doesn't need me to defend her. This is probably the dumbest thing she will ever read, if she even does. And I'm digging up old bones. But this is fresh for me. And it has become very personal. And Jen is more than just a good read for me these days. I actually somehow became a co-medienne and wrote a book. And through this strange chain of events, she is now my friend . . . in real life.

We even went on tour together last summer. I brought the ridiculous, and she brought the word of inspiration. We lived on a bus together. I saw her when she gracefully rolled out of her bunk before she'd brushed her hair or her teeth. I've watched her eat Mediterranean at midnight even though I don't agree that this is among her finer life choices. I've heard the stories. And she's good. She's not aching over any lost rela-tionships because of disagreement. She's not hurting anymore over threats and hateful words . . . but I am.

I'm just now starting my process, as a forty-three-year-old woman, of trying to figure out what I really believe—which hills I'm willing to die on. And the thought of getting burned at the stake and crucified publicly for things I believe in wholeheartedly (especially if those beliefs are in support of other human beings) is absolutely dumbfounding to me. I have been faced head-on with comments like "If you get linked back to Jen Hatmaker, it could hurt your witness." Why, though? And what does that mean, anyway? I hurt my witness because her beliefs go against the Christian norm? But has her boat-rocking, nay, her decision to love and fight for humanity, made her life invalid? Does it negate the work she has done to help thousands upon thousands of women to be released from baby prison? Does the thread she's now weaving unravel all she's done to encourage women everywhere? I, for one, welcome the call to question the Christian norm. I question the call of legalism. I question the lines that have been blurred between politics and religion, church and state. I question the truths I believe and why I believe them. I want to grow and be challenged and be forced to define my beliefs. I like the pushback.

Jen has been the center of a lot of controversy, but here's what she's been to me in the short time I've known her. She's been life. A breath of fresh air. During those few weeks of touring, I watched her embrace people she's never met like they were her own family. I watched her value the people she works with, answer questions from crowds with grace, candor, and conviction. I watched her get up early and work and motivate thousands of women in all stages of life night after night—out of her own past hurt and joy and experiences. One of those women being me.

She spoke so many words of life into me. She has encouraged me as a writer, a comedienne, a singer. She has listened to me talk about all that is shaking me as if she had nowhere to be, and she has, most important, let me know that it's OK. It's OK to be on a journey, and it's right to try to figure it all out for myself, and it's OK if I'm not there yet. She casts no judgment, knowing we're all human. She lives a life of love without resentment. She takes what has been done to her and lives a life of opposition to that very thing that tried to define her and take her out. She loves anyway. And I love her. We are cut from the same human cloth, and when we stand on the stage together, we stand as sisters. We are there with purpose, to unify, not divide. She taught me that—that our love for each other as women (and men) has nothing to do with agreeing or disagreeing.

To some of you, she is a bona fide celebrity, and she used to be that to me, too. I looked up to her because she was putting into words how I felt. She was a woman with kids on her hip and worldviews on her lips. She had the courage to express her feelings about the season of child-rearing that we both were in when I was just too afraid to admit that I was struggling. She was a picture of real vulnerability. How could a woman be so free to be so raw and honest about real life? Real feelings. Real pain. Real opinions. That is what courage looked like to me. Never in a million years did I think I could call her a friend, but she's just like you and me. She has lots of words, and she is using her gift just like we all should be doing.

So what I'm saying is this: I hope to be half the woman Jen Hatmaker is (in a few months) when I'm her age. Find your Jen Hatmaker. Find your example of someone who stands for truth and justice. Someone who fights for the underdog. Find your forerunner who sparks you to blaze your own trail.

And I want to honor God's greatest commandment: love. When they bury my body in an Amazon Prime box or scatter my ashes in London and Paris where I can finally be at rest, I just want people to remember that I loved well. If they remember me as an activist, a good leader, a funny lady . . . that's great. But I want to be remembered the way I remember my granny. The way I'll remember Jen Hatmaker when she inevitably dies of old age before me. I want to give out what has been poured into my life by some amazing women. I want to also take the hurt I have received from others and love anyway. It's so simple and difficult at the same time, but I'm convinced it's what leads to our internal peace.

Like every good nondenominational church slogan, here's what I've come to: Love God, and love people. Everything else is just extra.

HOT GLUE AND MATHEMATICS

If you have a jar in your house filled with thousands of old buttons, you are my kind of people. And don't ask me what I am going to do with all of those buttons until you can fully appreciate each of the buttons I have collected in this jar. Buttons from my granny's wool coat. Buttons from vintage blouses. Buttons from shirts older than me. Heck, I buy things at Goodwill just for the buttons.

See, what you don't know about me is that I am crafty. I may look like I prefer to spend hours in Crate & Barrel, but my love language is hot glue. I am a modern-day Picasso with a glue gun in my hand. When burlap was all the rage, I may as well have worn a "May I Help You?" vest to the local Michael's craft store, because I was there all the time. Basically, what I am trying to tell you is that my initials are DIY. Even as I write this, I am sitting here staring at a lampshade that I think could get a little flair from some burlap, buttons, and hot glue.

I am the friend you want around when the wedding decorator is a no-show on your big day. When the silk ribbon needs draping across the two-hundred-year-old mahogany railing in the church, I can steal the twist ties off the caterer's bread bags to make it happen. You need me to handle the flowers? I can snap twigs out of the yard and arrange them with flowers from Kroger to make your reception look like a million bucks.

Craftiness has taken me far in life. I have told you that I dipped my toe into the pageant world when I was young. And by dipped my toe, I mean I was in and out of there just long enough to win a pageant wearing a dress held up by rubber bands. The dress was too long, and I would surely trip on it and embarrass my family and hometown for years to come. So my mama did what any Southern woman would do: she bunched up the bottom of my A-line pageant gown to make handmade rosettes with RUBBER BANDS. It was magical. It made me a believer. And I won that beauty pageant. I became the enemy of contestants 3 through 16, but I didn't care. My mama didn't care. Maybe that is what won that pageant. If this story doesn't belong in a Hallmark movie, I don't know what does.

When you are a preteen and your legs are outgrowing your wardrobe, you have to be innovative. My great-grandmother's recommendation? Let's add some lace to the bottom—you can start a new trend. Not in 1989 you can't. But she won. And I wore lace on the bottom of my Lee jeans to a middle-school dance. Once. I only wore the jeans once.

Thanks to my artistic prowess, I am also an interior designer. In the '90s, we learned how to do our own interior design with stencils, and we learned how to create stamped wall borders. I have helped my mom stamp walls with brown paper bags, half a potato, and sponges cut into the shapes of ducks. We didn't think about the fact that the ducks might show up in years to come under a coat of new paint. At just the right angle of sunlight, you can see that stamped border of ducks around my childhood bedroom thirty years later.

I have mended the sole of my broken sandal with a staple gun on the way to a job interview and fixed my blown-out flip-flop on the way to the beach . . . while driving . . . with one knee. Ponytail holder break? I can reconfigure a paper clip to get your hair off your sweaty neck in an instant. Hole in your black leggings? Give me a Sharpie.

I've painted crappy furniture and made it fashionably distressed. I've painted vases to make them look like my grandmother's mercury glass. I have handmade more birthday gifts for my friends than I can count—journals, jewelry, headbands. I've wrapped them all and made the gift tag, too! I have even painted the Formica countertops in my kitchen. I will never do it again, but I am here to testify. All of this was before Pinterest was a thing. Ladies like me teach Pinterest how to hot-glue!

One of my favorite traditions around the holidays is to invite a group of ladies over for food (mostly festive dishes that involve cream cheese and bacon), and we are required to bring homemade ornaments for everyone. So if twelve are coming, you bring twelve homemade ornaments, and you leave with twelve new ornaments for your Christmas tree. We have had hand-sewn creations and ornaments made from toothpicks, felt balls, pipe cleaners, and pottery, and one even welded a Christmas tree ornament from rebar. And as the day of the party inches closer, it becomes quite a competition. Women are texting threats to each other and bragging about their own creations. *You are all going down. My ornament is the best yet.*

You just wait. Tracey, if you show up with premade crap from Walmart, you will not be invited back next year. You will be voted off the island. Get it together. I'm telling you, this was serious crafting business. You know what I showed up with every year? Burns. Burns on my fingers from the hot-glue gun. But is it worth it? You bet your googly eyes it is.

Women in the South are either born into the crafting world or indoctrinated soon after birth with all things Hobby Lobby. We learn crafting at home and at Vacation Bible School. We then mature into bubble letters and monograms around the time of puberty—when a young girl decides she has become woman enough for her very own hot-glue gun. We get married and have children and turn our crafting skills into survival skills on a shoestring budget.

Crafting is the second commandment for Southern women, behind mastering Granny's cornbread recipe in an iron skillet—a perfectly seasoned ironed skillet. My hot-glue gun stays plugged in, around the clock. Every good woman knows how to make a new throw pillow with an old T-shirt and some stitch-witchery. I guess when you can't afford the newest trends at HomeGoods, you have to take matters into your own hands. The options are: I can buy a new lamp for fifty dollars, or I can bedazzle the one I've got and make it one of a kind, call it "boho" (also for fifty dollars). You know it's true. I have more value in my crafting supplies than I do in my retirement account. School projects? Have no fear. Church carnival? On it. My child needs to dress like a celebrity for Spirit Week at school? *Son, do you know who Liberace is?*

Everything and everybody needs an update every once in a while. Can we all just pause and raise our hands in holy gratitude that we all moved beyond the '80s bangs, Rave hairspray, and Sun In? If you have no idea what I am talking about, then may I suggest you find one of your closest friends and ask them a simple heartfelt question: "Is she making fun of me?" If your hair looks like it has hot glue IN it, then yes, I am talking about you.

Do you ever watch the Ambush Makeover on the *Today* show? It's the highlight of my week. It gives me life. Those folks start off their day looking like a hobo who has never looked in the mirror, wearing a sweatshirt, not a stitch of makeup, and half-permed hair. They get snatched up and cleaned up, and then they are simply stunning. It's like they have never seen the cover of a magazine in the checkout line at Kroger. *I know you people have eyeballs. Can you not see that you may be a little washed up and need an update? How do you not know that your faded Columbia fleece is not flat-*

tering on you? What is keeping you from investing in a little touch-up here and there? Get out your Caboodles, girls! It is time. And if you can't do it for yourself, I'll call my friend, Carson Kressley. He will have you fixed up faster than you can say "Get a Room."

We all need to update ourselves and our lifestyle occasionally. Look around and take an inventory to decide what needs a little fixing up. We can even apply this to the relationships in our lives. Sometimes we need to help each other do a little updating. Have someone push us out of our comfort zone. We all need to take some time to hot-glue some glitter on our weaknesses until they get mistaken for strengths. I remember a trip to Vegas with some girlfriends where we took hours in our hotel room to get ready for a concert. All of us were moms. All of us were tired, faded moms. We put on fake lashes. Flashy clothes. We did it up right. Just like we used to do on Thursday nights in college before hitting the town. It was fun to play in each other's makeup bags and use ungodly amounts of hairspray. We couldn't maintain that schedule during our everyday lives, but it was fun to remember and learn some trade secrets from our friends. It was fun to feel like ourselves again—even if it involved cosmetics. If you grew up in the South, then you have probably been told by your mother, "Everyone feels better with a little lipstick on." And I agree that it's true.

A little improvement never hurt anybody. Except when you are dating. YOU CANNOT BEDAZZLE MEN. Do not try this at home. Do not find a guy who needs a little spit shine and think you can change him, dress him up, and call him unique. Lampshades work like that, humans don't.

There is no amount of hot glue on this earth that can fix a lack of integrity. You can't cover his character in glitter and make it shine. You can't crochet the holes in his dishonesty and make a scarf out of it. You can't take his cheap self and make him act top dollar. You can't use paper clips to hold his morals together. You can't spray-paint a romantic desire for him to pursue you the way you ought to be pursued. You can't papier-mâché good habits on him. You can't just send these things into the beauty shop (or the plastic surgeon) and expect a miracle like Honey Boo Boo's Mama June. Oh, you can try. I think every woman I know has missionary dated at least once. Don't missionary date. You can't change him. And you surely can't change where he comes from. You can try. He may change for a short bit to get your attention or to get you to believe in him. But at the end of the day, those parts of him you don't like are still there. They are just buried in colorful papier-mâché.

When a guy picks you up for a blind date in a souped-up Camaro that has the naked lady-devil decal on the back window, you should know that this man is not going to be a project. He is unchangeable. He has settled in. Now, the high school version of Heather would have been all about that sports car. But the Heather in her forties is not really into street racing anymore, ya know? When said Camaro driver also proceeds to use a buy one, get one half-off coupon at a nice restaurant and then takes you to play Goofy Golf, where he also uses a BOGO coupon for extra arcade tickets, he is probably not the level of maturity that you want to go around trying to fix. He is the blind date you just count your losses on. He is the guy you let get away. So take the gift he's given you and RUN.

There's the guy who called me by the wrong name during the first two hours of our date. Cut me some slack here; he looked like Bradley Cooper. He didn't need much fixin' on the outside, but not only was he insecure, he was as boring as a pile of hammers on the inside. *Could I build a life on just looking at him? Can he just sit there and be pretty? Could I endure a life of boredom with this joker?* No amount of pretty could make him interesting. No amount of refurbishing could help his personality.

If you listen closely to a girlfriend describe her new man, she will point out his flaws by how she describes him. Listen carefully. The traits she makes excuses for are the ones that scare her to death. They usually say things like "You can't help who you love" or "We're different. People don't understand our love." Slap this friend in the face. Be that friend. Because she needs to know that her rule book isn't different. Her rule book has the same math problems of generations of women before us. While it used to be said, "Oh, she will make a good man out of him," I am going to call the bluff of whoever said that. It's pure propaganda. It was probably said by a woman wearing an apron in a kitchen that smelled of pound cake while her husband was still at "the office."

I'm no mathematician here, but I have heard that healthy relationships are a multiplication problem, not addition. In a good relationship, $1 \times 1 = 1$. Each person must bring his or her whole self into the equation. The problem comes in when we bring our whole 1 into the relationship and the other does not. That's where we get out the crafting supplies and try to work the magic. Unfortunately, relationships aren't made of flair and makeovers. They aren't simple addition. If they were, then $1 + 0 = 1$, and I could be totally in control of the outcome of the relationship. Lord knows, I have tried that math problem, and it tested more like calculus. No matter what my past boyfriends or ex-husband did, I would make up for it. The less they put into the relationship, the harder I would work to make sure it looked good and acceptable on the outside.

We try to figure out what he wants, and we do everything in our power to provide it for him. Our hope is to salvage the connection. But it will not work. No matter how much we try, we can't change him. No matter how many stamped borders she puts on his walls, his house is still condemnable.

If he's a big fat zero, then the relationship will be a big fat zero. And there is nothing you can do about it. Put down your hot-glue gun and step away. You can pray, hope, plead, and do everything in your power to get him to see the light, but you can't change him. And more important, you can't make up for whatever he lacks. No matter how great you become, 10×0 is still 0.

Quit trying to work that math problem, girl. What you've got is a real problem. It may not feel like a problem when you are first dating, but as that relationship turns serious, there comes a point where you just have to face the facts.

If you think you might be in love with a zero, here are some tips for you. Ask a friend, and avoid denial. You want the relationship to work. You really do. He is cool. He is a musician. He is funny. My God, he is funny. And it's really easy to deceive yourself. But he is still a zero in this equation. He can barely hold down a job, his emotions are all over the place, and he still lives with his parents. Listen to your friends who are honest about him. They see things you don't because you are blinded by love.

And when you know the truth and finally see the light, be willing to walk away. You know the old saying "If you love something, set it free. If it comes back, it's yours; if not, it was never meant to be"? Well, that is a terrible idea, because a lot of times the zero in the relationship comes back over and over again. And he will keep coming back. You have to learn how to lock your door and close the blinds.

Regardless of the crafting skills you possess, there is no amount of fixing up that can be done on a man you love. You can try. You can dust him off, get him prepped, and start painting on him like a fresh canvas. You can take an old boring lamp and embellish the lampshade to make it suit your taste. You're not really changing the lamp itself. It is still there in its original form. It is still an old fire hazard with knobs missing. You haven't changed the foundation. You've just put lipstick on the pig.

Burlap gets dusty. Glitter is annoying. It's always cheaper in the long run to just buy the real thing. The one that is beautiful from the beginning. The lamp that doesn't need anything added to it to make it work. It fits perfectly in the perfect spot in your house. So save your time and money for the real thing. It won't disappoint. And for the love, step away from the glue gun.

8

JUNK DRAWER

Where are the matches? I need to get off this couch and find some matches to light one of the 143 candles I have in my house. Why am I always looking for the matches? I know I got some from that new little Italian restaurant down the street. If a restaurant has free matches, I am a fan. I will take a pack every time I am there. Why? Because I need to throw them in my junk drawer with all the other boxes of matches. *Oh, you have one, too? Of course you do. We all have THAT junk drawer.*

I dig around in this godforsaken drawer, and while I am looking for matches, I find 8,649 other things I forgot I had. My hand gets tangled in fishing line, a staple gun falls out on my toes, and the thing I am looking for is buried under every sharp object I have ever owned. I get stabbed and entangled all at the same time. Then I unexpectedly find a random stack of photos and casually slip into forty-five minutes of reminiscing over pictures of my kids that I haven't seen in ten years. Tears start flowing, and if my ovaries are still working, they are aching. Maybe it's cramps. I'm sure there's a Midol in here somewhere.

What kinds of skeletons do you have hanging out in your junk drawer? I knocked over a box of Hot Tamales and eventually threw the box away but didn't have the patience to clean out the millions of candies that are floating around in junk-drawer utopia. I have an old elbow brace—because who knows where that goes? Never played a day of tennis in my life, so not sure what that is about. Elbow braces and ankle wraps don't really belong in the medicine cabinet, but where do they belong? No one knows. I have old cell phone chargers from 1999, just in case they come back around. Breathe Right strips in their crushed box because the dry air in Colorado prevented my nose from functioning properly. You would think they would make their way to my bedside table, but that is too much walking. I have felt pads to put on the legs of my dining chairs so they will stop scratching my wood floors, but it's apparently too much work for me to get down on my hands and knees to peel and stick those things because I may not get back up. I have bedsheet clips that came in a six-pack. Mattresses have four corners, yet I have two extra in case I want them to double as garter clips, I guess. Oh, and look, here's some of those corn-on-the-cob holders. You know the ones. Then I find odd-sized batteries that I was looking for two months ago. And there's my return-address monogram stamp (don't tell) for the letters that I don't write anymore because . . . it is 2020. My junk drawer is home to all the curly straws, the free dental floss from my dentist's office, a crusty old medicine syringe, and a few rubber bands that like to tangle everything together. There's a fine line between being resourceful and being a stage 5 hoarder who could be featured on that TLC show. I like to toe that line.

Now, if you are a real special kind of hoarder, you have enough crap to justify having a junk drawer in more than one room of your home. A bedroom's junk drawer is an extra-special place typically forbidden to guests and children. It basically has all the same stuff mentioned above. The only difference? That's none of your business.

These junk-drawer items are the honorable mention at the beauty pageant. They are the cake cutters at the wedding. They are the card table at Thanksgiving dinner. They enter the race, but they tucker out before the finish line. Speaking of . . .

In my junk drawer, I find the medal from that time I walked three miles in a 5K. WALKED. That doesn't deserve a medal, but it's 2020, and everyone gets medals . . . to stick in the junk drawer. Where else should I put it? If I hung it up, it might motivate me to walk three miles again, and I don't have any plans for that to happen. And all the stuff gets tangled up into a big ol' bird's nest. Speaking of nesting . . .

I love nesting. It ain't only for the pregnant people. I love organizing and rearranging, but I never touch that drawer. It's sacred. A sacred mess. I am getting ready to move again, closer to town, and purging all the things. If you had told me fifteen years ago that I would be getting rid of all my pewter serving pieces or my coffee table made out of a wooden pallet, I would have called you blasphemous. They were knit together with my soul. If you had told me ten years ago that I would be painting all my new walls white instead of bright colors, I would have told you to go get a life. No one paints walls white. Yep, they do in 2020. And they decorate with cactuses. Like the '70s all over again. And that, my friends, is why we never empty the junk drawer—you never know when you might need those items again.

I hold on to things that I haven't touched in years. I have moved these items from house to house over the course of a decade or more. I literally take the drawer out, dump it into a moving box, and label it "junk drawer." It's typically the last box I unpack. And by unpack, I mean, I just dump the box into the only drawer left empty in my new home.

The items in my junk drawer sometimes land there because I do not take the time to deal with them. If I took the time to place an item in a designated spot in my house, I would get sidetracked with having to reorganize all the other cabinets I have been putting off. It's just too much when you have your arms filled with grocery sacks and you just slipped on a piece of bologna on your tile floor. If I took the time to organize from the get-go, I wouldn't need this drawer.

In the spirit of tidiness, I would like to give a big *domo arigato* to Marie Kondo for tidying up all of our crap on Netflix and teaching us how to "spark joy" with the blue jeans from tenth grade that we can no longer fit into. It didn't bring me joy to purge them; it made me very, very angry that I used to be so skinny with very little effort. There's not enough Ex-Lax on planet Earth to get me back in those jeans. And tonight I have to sleep on the couch because all of my clothes are folded vertically on my bed, and there's no room left for me in the inn. Marie, can you help me purge the people in my life who no longer spark joy? Is there a life-size drop box at the Goodwill down the street, or should I call for a curbside pickup? I have lots of people who need to be purged; they'd better bring a big truck.

I once read that you should only keep items that fit into one of three categories: functional, meaningful, or beautiful. Marie Kondo's mantra kinda says the same thing, but not. Flashlights don't spark joy, Marie, but I need them to spark a light when a tornado knocks the power out. So they go in the junk drawer.

There's another kind of junk drawer that holds all the junk we aren't willing to face in our lives. We shove stuff in there with the best intentions to get around to it later. We hold on to items that we haven't used in years because we are afraid we might need them again one day. The contents of my junk drawer are all familiar to me—I can always depend on them being there, regardless of whether I need them or not. We have beautifully organized lives, but we have that one spot that is untouchable. We are the only ones allowed in there. We would be mortified if a stranger opened it and saw all the junk spill out.

What would happen if I cleaned out the junk and found a place for all of it? What if something landed safely in its rightful cabinet and I could retrieve it when I needed it?

Like that one friend who is toxic but we are afraid we might need one day. What about that bitterness, tucked way in the back, that we pull out when we just want to be mad? The old tapes of rejection that you pull out and pop in the player.

Quit sifting through that crap and just trash it. Forget recycling. Send that mess straight to the landfill. Put those Breathe Right strips in the bin, because they are cutting off your airflow. Fill that drawer with things you'll use. It is OK if they don't have their own space yet.

I have a junk drawer, too. We all do. We all have baggage.

Let's just help each other clean it out.

9

CLASS REUNIONS AND SPANX

This past weekend I went to my twenty-fifth high school reunion. I experimented with how many pair of Spanx I could realistically wear without turning blue. Sitting and breathing at the same time is not a requirement at that function per se. It's a lot easier to catch up while you are standing, so I had to be extra-Spanxed that night. And if my tight forehead and eyebrow wax didn't impress my old high school friends, then I should have just stayed home.

Who am I kidding here? Thanks to social media, there are no surprises at class reunions anymore. By the time you arrive, everyone is well aware of the valedictorian who turned into a full-fledged cat lady after her brief and unsuccessful run on *Jeopardy!* in '04. Bless. You have already seen pics of the former baseball player who is now fat and bald and divorced two times over. You already know who made it out of that town and who stayed to cheer on the high school football team for life. You know where the hoods and preps ended up. The highlight of all class reunions, of course, is to observe (and judge) those who have not aged so gracefully.

At my high school, all of the classes from previous decades join together for the class reunion opening ceremony. Everyone shows up in the same tired, wrinkled, and worn-out condition. We have no one to impress. Except that one girl from the class of 1984, the former cheerleader, who has worked so hard on her body that she can't wait for this shining moment. She gave herself away when she fell up the bleacher stairs during the opening celebration. Her inebriated state left nothing to the imagination when that bodycon dress rolled up like a miniblind. Her scars from the mommy makeover were on display for all the decades to witness.

At a twenty-five-year class reunion, we don't need a fancy event, a disc jockey, or a weekend full of things to do. Who has the energy or money for all that? We just want to hang out at TJ Mulligan's, catch up, and rehash those embarrassing stories from dances and senior parties. At your first reunion, ten years out of high school, everyone is still trying to impress people with their success. First marriages and fore-heads are still intact. But at twenty years and after, the frills are gone. We are all divorced, and our give-a-damn's busted. We all know who has been to rehab and who needs to go to rehab. Our false pretenses have gone away, and we are more authentic than we have ever been. We have all birthed babies, birthed careers, and birthed a series of bad decisions that have knocked down our need for approval from this group of historic friends whom we won't see for another decade.

Don't you love the catch-up game, though?

"Oh, you are a high school counselor now? I bet you are so good at that because of your experience with all of your personalities."

"What? You're a Realtor? Well, I guess selling houses is better than all them drugs you used to sell."

"You're a plumber now? Well, you did lay a lot of pipe back in the day."

"Byron Burns, I haven't seen you since you ran my car through the Medina Cemetery and busted up my vanity plate. Those were good times, Byron. Also, you owe me $14.92."

Growing up, there were five of us who did everything together—Heather, Sara, Ashley, Jennifer, and Amy. Could there be a list of girl names that is any more '90s? The answer is no. There is no mistaking what decade we came from. We did the slumber parties, rode "the strip," ditched our boyfriends to hang out. We were tried and true, besties for the restie. We were in each other's weddings. We even went on a senior trip together to the Bahamas and dubbed ourselves, henceforth and forevermore, "the Bahama Mamas." And for the record, this is the only group text I will ever be a part of.

The Bahama Mamas (sans Amy, who ditched us for a vacation in Mexico) made our debut at our small town's social event of the year—our twenty-fifth reunion. We already knew the who, what, when, and where of each other's lives. I mean, good Lord, there were only eleven total in our class at the reunion. It doesn't take long to cover all the details.

And of course, even though the Bahama Mamas were up to speed on each other's detailed life situations, we still found ourselves huddled up together like we were waiting on someone to ask us to dance. Minutes had turned to hours when it hit me. We are our parents. We are our mothers. We are old. We are everything we swore we would not be. Because we, the Bahama Mamas, just spent the last seventy-three minutes comparing surgeries and how many pills we eat on the daily. We have gone from comparing tanning creams to comparing

Aspercreme. From comparing torn jeans to torn ACLs. From Boone's Farm to the nut farm. The one thing that has stood the test of time is mastering the art of not getting pregnant. We all walked away winners in that category.

One of the BMs, with literal tears in her eyes, was telling us about her upcoming ablation. She knew it would be the expiration of her childbearing years. This mother of three was mourning the loss of the children she would never have. We were sucked into a full-on counseling session when her husband turned around and said, "What in the world are you talking about? I had a vasectomy ten years ago." So let me get this straight, you haven't been able to have a child in the last ten years, but tonight is the night you want to cry about it? Really? Right here in front of Johnny Scott?

Another BM sat there showing us her new condition where she bruises easily—she looked like she should have been in the class of '44, not '94. She had her shin wrapped because her dog brushed against her leg and left a bruise as big around as her homecoming crown.

The heroine of the night was double-fisting Diet Cokes while the rest of us were face-pounding champagne. If I had been through the hell she had walked through the last three years, I would have skipped rehab and gone straight to the big house. Her sobriety was locked down tighter than my geometry teacher's face-lift. She *would* have won story of the night. But guess who brought it home for the win?

Me and my hemorrhoids.

I looked at those three heifers and said, "Every single one of y'all can shut up, because I just had hemorrhoid surgery. Take a seat . . . because I can't. Until you have had women in your church sign up to bring you casseroles because your anus is burning like a homecoming bonfire, don't talk to me. Where was your casserole? Where were you on the 'back end' when I needed you most? Where were you when this was going down and my surgeon was going up? Not a single one of y'all helped adjust my donut—I could have used some donuts. In high school, I held your hair back when you were throwing up, and you can't even empty out my catheter bag? You don't have a story. Your life and untouched a-hole are irrelevant. You don't even get to sit at my table anymore. You keep on working your twelve-step program, because I can't even take twelve steps. Awwwwweeeee, so sorry about your shin bruise, but the biggest bruise here is on my ego." What story you got, Amy? I am sorry you were in Mexico and couldn't make it to our medical seminar. My story wins the night—so don't even bother.

Going to a high school reunion makes me reflect on how I thought life was going to be. And good Lord, it makes me laugh at all the things I didn't know. Strolling the school hallways that still smelled like a mixture of pine-scented bathroom cleaner and the rectangle pizza being served in the cafeteria that day. Peeking into the library where the elementary book fair went down each year—the most educational thing I can recall from elementary school. I thought the purpose of a book fair was to encourage me to read. No, it was to teach kids the crushing reality of being on a budget. *Welcome to adulthood, little girl, you can't afford these sticker books. Go back to class.* Also, I would like to take the time to say congratulations to all the recent high school graduates out there for making it through the easiest time of your life. Some of you may feel like it is the end of your life. It is. The end of your good life—living at home for free, someone feeding you and doing your laundry. You will never have this again. So congratulations, you have been set free into a world of hard work, paying bills, and picking up your own prescriptions when you are deathly ill. We tricked you; it's not fun out here at all.

Going to a high school reunion also means a brief weekend stay at the house I grew up in. And if you are as lucky as I am, your parents' house will be like an Airbnb stay on Memory

Lane. Why in the world can't we update the childhood pics on the bedside table or just relocate them? It's like staying in an old dusty hotel where all the black-and-white photos are of people you know. A dreamy vacay destination, really.

Every time I visit my parents, I learn about their friends who have gotten good news about their recent colonoscopies and who have recently checked in at the funeral home.

"Mom, how do you know all of this stuff? Do you just sit around and read the obituaries all day?"

"No, Heather, we signed up for notifications from the funeral home. It just pops up right here on my phone. See? I don't want to miss anyone's funeral. That would be awful."

Are you kidding me right now? I just died. I am dead. Did you get that notification?

First notification of the morning: *It's Betty Jean Winkle's birthday. Click here to wish her a happy birthday.*
Second notification: *Funeral arrangements for John Paul Honeycutt. Click here to send a green bean casserole to his grieving widow.*

You gotta hand it to that funeral home—they are using technology the way God intended it—"Recue the perishing, care for the dying, click here to send flowers." All in one fell swoop.

I admit, as I have aged, I have become a little more paranoid about my aging health. "Welcome to forty, I hope you like ibuprofen" was a birthday card I got from a cousin a few years ago when I went flying over that hill. He ain't lying. One of my favorite games to play is "Is my headache from too much caffeine, my headband, lack of vegetables, dehydration, or a brain aneurysm?" Probably the last. Most definitely.

Coco Chanel once said, "Nature gives you the face you have at twenty. It is up to you to merit the face you have at fifty." Well, if that is the case, I am not sure who is to blame for this face I have right now at forty-three. The ex? My teenage children? Or the stupid people at Walmart?

No, Coco, if I am lucky, science will allow me to drag this forty-three-year-old face into the spa and walk out looking twenty-nine over and over again. Look, I have never loved someone as much as I love my esthetician. She is my soul mate, who will never let me look as old as I feel. She comes at me with those needles, and I can't say no. If my kids have to starve, so be it. Take all my money, and take all my wrinkles with it.

Look, I don't know how it happens. One day, you are twenty-five, staying up until three A.M., eating pizza and watching movies. The next day, you are forty-three, eating kale, and you pull a muscle in your back putting on your socks. At what age do I start storing my leftovers in Country Crock butter tubs? When do I start licking my fingers to turn the pages in a book? I feel like that is a pretty significant aging marker. And fellas, I feel like life should change a little for you when you hit your forties, too. It's time to leave them young girls alone and get you a woman who understands the signs of a stroke.

If I am up late and an infomercial is on, get my credit card. I am ordering all the natural remedies that QVC has to sell. I am watching all the natural skin-care infomercials that Christie Brinkley endorses. Whatever is good enough for the Uptown Girl is good enough for me. I will make all the concoctions with ingredients from my kitchen that supposedly help you age gracefully. And if you rub three drops of olive oil and Epsom salts on a painful spot on your body, it will immediately feel greasier and saltier. Works every time. Doesn't make me feel any younger but definitely makes a great salt scrub in the bath.

Being over forty doesn't seem as bad as it used to. Life isn't over. Look at Ellen. Look at Sofía Vergara. Julia Child wrote her first cookbook at forty-nine. Martha Stewart published *Entertaining* at forty-one. J. K. Rowling published *Harry Potter* when she was in her forties. Then there's Meryl Streep and Oprah, who are killing it in their later years. And we can't even touch Jenny from the block. She is on fire but not from hemorrhoids.

Don't worry, beauty is on the inside, not the outside. Riiiiiight. My insides aren't beautiful, either. My liver is two pills short of being pickled. What's left of my intestines has a thick coating of laxative sludge on the inside. My lungs have never smoked, but they have sucked in enough hairspray to style Tammy Faye Bakker for her casket. And the spots on my skin? I earned every single one of them. When your boyfriend has a tanning bed in his home, your perception of what a good tan looks like gets a little skewed. I was never dark enough. By the time prom season rolled around, all you could see of me was the whites of my eyes and my teeth. Still wouldn't wear a light-colored dress because it might "wash me out." Thank goodness for modern medicine and dermatology.

Are the notifications from the funeral home just an inevitable part of life? Do those things just come with aging, like hemorrhoids come with childbirth? I suppose the older we get, the more loss we experience, and the more illness we see, the more fear digs its spiked heels into our minds. The one thing that scares me the most is becoming a chronic worrier. That woman who can barely leave her home because she is afraid of the danger in everything. That never looks good on anybody. I think we moms get hit the worst, no doubt. Most of us moms are conditioned by all the years of rearing children. I think it is an uphill battle for the rest of our lives. We carry the concern and fear around our necks like medallions. As I grow older and wiser, I want to see life through a lens of gratitude for my own blessings. I want to see each day as a gift even if it doesn't always feel that way. I want to serve others from a place of love and generosity, not a place of fear and panic for my own family's health.

When I think about what I want to become in the years ahead of me, I focus on the word "become." I think most people think that they have already arrived in their forties and fifties, and they plan to coast to retirement. I have no intention of collecting seashells on the seashore in twenty or thirty years. I want to keep becoming. I want to continue evolving. I want to live new experiences and keep contributing to this big ol' world.

There's a certain entitlement you carry with you when you have a little bit of age under your belt. People give you more grace to say and do what you want. You aren't afraid to make decisions, others' opinions of you carry less importance, and if you are lucky, you have a little bit of a nest egg to spend on yourself and others. I hope that my biggest goal isn't vanity. Wasting time worrying about wrinkles instead of character. Why can't we handle them both? Take care of our bodies so that we feel good but also focus on making others feel good. I don't think it is one or the other. I think I will do both.

I think aging gives you permission to live with intentionality. Less to achieve, less to prove, more to give back. That is a beautiful thing. Women aren't allowed to age in our society. Men are. And that ticks me off. The burden of having to be everlastingly beautiful is a heavy one. But the narrative on beauty can change. Here's the truth: women grow more powerful with age, and our culture does not find power attractive in a woman. Let's not throw out our makeup bags but find a way to toss out the beauty standards that devalue us. It's some kind of balance for us ladies between fighting it and accepting it that requires a great deal of grace and courage. Courage— there's that word again.

I don't know what is ahead of me. We aren't promised tomorrow. I want to live a long, beautiful, hemorrhoid-free life with my family and friends. I have lots of fears about aging and screwing it up. All I know is that I don't want to die alone in my house with a bunch of cats. So for now, I will drink more water, eat less sodium, and wear sunscreen. But I would rather wear pantyhose with my bathin' suit at the Fourth of July pool party than wear one of those beekeeper sunscreen hats on the beach. Naw, I ain't doin' it.

10

SWEET TOOTH

The year was 2015 when I realized I had a problem. I had done my research and plotted my next steps. I knew where to get my next hit. I knew I had to go to Denver to get it. The thought of it made my heart race and kept me awake at night. I just couldn't let it go. It was the chase. It was all about rebellion for me. I knew I would disappoint some people in my life, but it was worth it. This wasn't the first time, and I knew it wouldn't be the last time. I just didn't know it would cost me so much.

I'm talking about the wild chase for macaroons. And Denver has some of the best.

It was a good idea at first. My Pinterest board supported this decision, and there was no way to change my mind. A cute little cookie that all the French rave about. My friends were making them, and I never knew what I was missing out on until I tried that little raspberry cookie. And I will never be the same.

Anybody else out there have a sweet tooth? Good grief. I could eat a full spread at Fogo de Chão and still walk away craving a molten lava cake from Domino's. It's the thorn in my side—sugar. I wish I could tell you that I'm addicted to kale or kombucha, but God did not gift me with a hunger for a healthy constitution.

Another addiction that is telling my story right now is the ambient sound of a cardboard box landing on my front doorstep. (My doorbell literally just rang as I wrote this.) You know the sound I am referring to. Amazon Prime, you are the lover of my soul. You get me. You know exactly how to meet my needs, and you are never, ever late—even on the Sabbath. You take my procrastination and deliver on time, every time. You fill the cracks in my spirit. I can't live a day without you and never plan to. That's like saying I could live another day without those woven baskets and new nine-by-thirteen Pyrex baking dishes I just ordered. That's like saying I could live without HGTV or Instagram. I used to want to be cremated upon death, but as of late, I've decided I want to be buried in an Amazon Prime box. You can keep your gift wrap, AP, but fold up those corners and let my lifeless body be at peace within your four walls.

Dear Poshmark, you, too, are a temptation to my pocketbook. I have prayed day and night for my love of gently used goods to go away. I cut my teeth on garage sales and thought I had moved on, but now this. This is the way to satisfy my longing for name brands at reduced prices. You are worse than cupcakes, you temptress. I could've lived three lifetimes without buying those used Steve Maddens, but I just couldn't say no. Thanks for nothing (everything), Poshmark.

There are a lot of things I love, but my single greatest infatuation is reserved only for one. You have won my heart and my paycheck, Free People. It's always been you. There's just something about us. And you have a way of communicating that is second to none. I can be having the worst day and be convinced that I don't need one more pair of jeans, but you always know just what to say to change my mind. And yes, I do need them in four different colors. Thank you! How did you know, Free People?

Don't you judge me.

And because they run big, I can order a size smaller than I really am, and let's face it, if you have the choice between buy-

ing something that makes you feel skinny and buying something two numerical sizes larger, you know which one you
are going to choose! Every. Dang. Time. I am a faithful Free
People customer. I am one purchase away from . . . *On the
next episode of* Hoarders*: We have a single mom who kicked out
two teenage children to make room for her shopping addiction.*
The only downside to Free People: they're anything but free.

I also may or may not have recently acquired an innocent
addiction to Botox. I'm talking just the slightest dependence.
I also may or may not have an addiction to watching *Sister
Wives*. I just can't look away.

How about my addiction to watching shows about addiction? Is that a real thing? I bet this is a diagnosis. It's its own
episode.

Yes, in fact, it is. TLC has tapped into that weird part of
our brains that makes us watch these shows without fail. *My
600-Lb. Life* and *My Strange Addiction* are my secret obses-
sions. It is, no doubt, the train wreck that I can't stop watching. The girl who eats sand. The couple who is addicted to
coffee enemas. I get you. I see you. I am with you.

I get so involved emotionally with these characters, and
they have no idea I exist. If they only lose one hundred pounds
at their first checkup, I'm upset and yelling at the television.

"PUT IN THE WORK, DEBORAH! YOU ARE WORTH MORE!" Um. She just lost one hundred pounds, and I (the television audience of one) am ticked off. *I have supported you and cheered for you and you must not want it as badly as I do, Deborah!* Or how about the ones who don't lose a single pound? I'm over here starving myself for this two-hour episode so you don't feel alone, just for you to blame your third cousin twice removed for the fact that you can't break your addiction to mashed potatoes!?!

Forget you, Barry!

Addiction is nothing to joke about. If anybody realizes this, it's me. *Also note: I am eating two packs of Nutty Buddies while I am writing this.* Addiction is real. Addiction is life-altering. Addiction is a monster.

Although I like to make light of my adult addiction to Ryan Reynolds or my teenage addiction to tanning beds, I do know the heaviness of dependence. I grew up with addiction in my family. I also know that exposure to addiction is partly to blame for my warped sense of humor. There has to be some real sophisticated scientific data out there to show that children who grow up around addiction turn out really funny and sarcastic 100 percent of the time. Now you know. Humor is my coping mechanism of choice. (That and dark chocolate.) I learned to laugh and make jokes when I was young because things weren't always funny. I was hurting, and laughter truly was my medicine. It was also my distraction.

I've had to turn other people's mistakes into my responsibility since I can remember. I have seen the relentless loss and destruction addiction can cause. I have also seen the redemption and reconciliation that can bloom from it, too.

This is a sensitive subject and one that I don't talk about lightly. I have gone back and forth and lost nights of sleep debating whether or not to share. I've cried at the thought of hurting other parties with the written truth, but it's just that—the truth. And it's part of my story.

I grew up in addiction. It was in my home, and it was "normal." It was all I knew. Not only did I grow up watching it and being deeply affected by it, but I grew up being taught by others to enable it. I was taught that I had a part to play in how good or bad this thing was gonna get. I was taught to walk on eggshells, to be good, to stay out of the way. To do more. To do less. And if I could, in fact, do and be all of these things, then all would be well . . . until the next time when it wasn't. If I could toe the line, then not only would I make things better for the abuser and for myself, but I would make life better for other people who were closely affected by this addiction, too. It was up to me. Talk less. Smile more. You can do it.

Life was wonderful and full in many ways. I had amazing friends and life events that kept me busy and happy(ish). My sweet granny did most of the heavy lifting when it came to my heart and emotions. If it hadn't been for her, I might be addicted to cocaine, not Coke Zero. She kept life stable when it was falling apart.

During my life in the pressure cooker, I became programmed to absorb the needs of everyone around me. I was trained to stay. To fix. To work harder. And I was trained that you don't leave.

We lay down our lives for others. We make everyone else a priority. I became the peacemaker at all cost. Whatever it takes, make it happen: peace. I was in charge. It was up to me. I never caused any trouble, because I was too busy learning to take ownership and blame for the mistakes of others.

I became the mother, the father, the judge, and the jury. I became the bailiff, holding the keys (or so I thought) that would set the prisoner free. It is codependency at its finest: *I will care about you more than you care about yourself.* I was a pro at one-sided relationships where I met all the emotional and self-esteem needs. Expending all of my energy meeting the needs of others. Never saying "no" or "enough."

After walking an extremely long road as a casualty of others' addictions, I learned that we are not responsible for fixing anyone but ourselves. In fact, we can't. We cannot make changes for someone else. They have to put in the work. They do. We don't own their choices. They do. Do I need to say that again? LET THEM OWN THEIR CHOICES. Remember that toolbox I mentioned that I carried into adulthood? My toolbox that I drag around with me everywhere in order to fix people? Well, there are not enough tools in there to accomplish anything. Because we do not have the tools to fix someone else's problems. They don't sell those down at the Home Depot. The only tools we can possess are the ones to fix our own stuff.

Please know this: I am so saddened by addiction. I am not hard-hearted toward the life issues and circumstances that cause addictions in the first place. I don't blame or hate. I know it is not easy out there. I know that pain is hard. We are broken. We get broken. We are victims. We are villains. We experience loss. We experience abandonment. We have seasons of feast and famine. All of us. It's all just really hard. While your story may look different from another's, we are all doing the best we can with the tools we have.

When all we are ever served is a full helping of brokenness, it's all we know how to give. She's broken, so she breaks others. He's broken, so he breaks others. Accepting the pardon and living our destiny and purpose are not easy, but they are a choice.

I love people, and I love to give. This is my real addiction. I might as well face it, I'm addicted to love. (You just started singing it, didn't you?) Gotta admit that Robert Palmer music video with his swaying red-lipped female guitarists goes down as one of the most memorable music videos of my childhood. Addiction to loving people is not a bad thing, right? Except, I was addicted to *fixing* people and calling it love.

Giving until there's nothing left. I have worn it like a badge of honor. Taking on burdens and weaknesses and making them mine. I would try them on for size and see if they fit on my shoulders nicely. I was trained for this. It is a blurry line for Christ followers. It is a mixed bag of opinions on this subject of self-sacrifice. My heart says to love people without hesitation. But I finally learned that unconditional love didn't require unconditional staying. (Pause here because I feel like someone might need to read that again.) Unconditional love does not require unconditional staying.

Loving someone who has hurt you or has the potential to hurt you comes with boundaries—a word I was not taught in Sunday school. Sure, I learned how to spell Shadrach, Meshach, and Abednego, but I never learned a dang thing about how to protect my heart and how to not fall into a self-destructive life of becoming an empath.

What is an empath? We are a special breed. We are highly attuned to other people's moods, and we feel everything deeply and extremely. We are nurturers. We are healers. We feel everything, and we absorb the pain and stress of others. It is exhausting. It took a lot of pain for me to understand my tendencies and habits. It took lots of self-reflection to realize that setting a boundary was the only thing that would protect me. I can't be trusted to protect myself. To establish boundaries, I had to be clear about my beliefs, values, and limits. Boundaries require me to prioritize myself and find my own voice.

Boundaries are powerful. Knowledge is power. So is counseling. Bless my counselor. She can have all my money and my house, too. She helped me realize that I am not the first person and I won't be the last person who has experienced the same behaviors. To hear someone say, "You aren't the only person hurting here," flipped a switch for me. An empath feels others' pain, remember? She shifted my perspective on what I thought other people owed me. She helped me lower some of my emotional expectations of others but raise expectations for myself and my life. She filled my toolbox with what I needed for me and took out the tools I have been carrying around since my childhood to fix everybody else.

In a weird way, it feels so much better to learn there is a name for you—to learn that your behavior is listed in a psychology book out there. I am textbook. As much as I would like to think of myself as unique, there I am, a carbon copy of every other empath in the world. That knowledge really gave me power. Knowing the behaviors, the triggers, the slippery slope of my love addiction. That is powerful! That is the kind of power that takes your love and repositions it on the right person. I can now see that I learned some savvy grit and resilience that allowed me to take control of my own adult life circumstances. I don't believe I would have learned that as a young girl. As a female in the Bible Belt, you are taught by well-meaning people to get married, learn to cook, smile, nod, agree, be pretty, and everything will work out for you. But I want to teach my children to love well, to have healthy boundaries and stand up for truth and justice, and to stand up for themselves and say, "I ain't doin' it."

11

GETAWAY CAR

It's a quarter after two, and my partner in crime is on her way to pick me up. She is driving me downtown to the courthouse for a free legal consultation. She is driving instead of me because "I don't knowwwwww where it issssss." (*Whining.*) It's not like it's 2013 and I can't look up the address myself on Google Maps or anything. I really just needed a partner to shove me out of the car. I have never even gotten a speeding ticket, much less stepped one foot into a courthouse building. Metal detector? What? I gotta empty out my purse? Nope. I can't do this.

I'm sorry, Mr. Officer in gray polyester who has a stone face. I need to get out of this line and go back to my car, back to my apartment, and back to my marriage. Could you just excuse me and let me scoop up my wallet, lipstick, and tampons off this conveyor belt and act like this never happened? Thank you, good day, sir.

She grabbed my elbow and said, "Yes, you can. Look at all of these people. They are fighting battles much bigger than yours. If they can figure it out, so can you. Good Lord, Heather, people get divorced every single day. Keep walking." I had spent years ready to walk and start a new life, but until that day, I didn't know how heavy my shoes were.

The truth is, with each of those steps into that courthouse, I grew more and more courageous. Kinda like someone who is training for a marathon—I just had to take one step at a time until I reached my destination. I don't usually run unless I'm being chased. And even then, I might trip and play dead just to get out of running. But this race I couldn't avoid. I had played dead long enough.

We got back in her car with a stack of papers and some homework. I had multicolored sticky notes, multicolored highlighters, file folders, every office supply a girl might need to become Judge Judy. I became a mad researcher . . . *20 Smart Tips to Get through Your Divorce Hearing with Ease, How to Get a Divorce When You Are Broke* . . . Clicking on everything, every helpful hint, reading every word on every website about the procedures of divorce in the state of Colorado. I was ready for my legal career. I took a long, deep breath right there outside of that courthouse on Tejon Street. That deep breath was the beginning of the rest of my life. Then she drove me to Sonic for celebratory cherry limeades, because that is what real friends do! (Note: this was before I knew I liked wine. If I had known, that last sentence would have ended differently. Perhaps the whole day would have ended differently.)

It's like rolling someone's yard when you're in high school. You gotta delegate the responsible one who will keep a lookout for the cops—this is also the one who never leaves the car. Watching the surroundings, gripping the steering wheel at ten and two while the necessary work is being done outside of the vehicle, ready to call out and hit the gas pedal at the first sign of danger. The Transportation and the Security.

Months later, that same friend and the same getaway car drove me two hours north to the final day in court with my husband. She shopped while I divorced. She shopped for a replacement ring for my left hand. The divorce was a business transaction at this point. All the words had been said, all the tears had been cried, and all the shattered dreams were on their way to the emergency room for stitching up. All that was left to figure out was the money. Seriously. That's what it came down to. Who pays the money, and who gets the goldfish? We had two kids to support, and I had $78.12 to my name. One hour, in and out. Signed on the dotted line. I got back into my getaway car, and it was over. Then we had a burger and fries. Possibly a milkshake.

I make it sound easy, don't I? Well, I was still in no shape to drive. I was just sitting there staring out the windshield. The kind of stare you see in a country music video. While she drove, I just kept saying, "I am divorced? I am divorced. Divorced. The big D. Just like that, divorced. Now I have to check a new box on my taxes."

When you are babbling on and on in a state of PTSD, you need a driver. Who is going to deliver you safely from point A to point B when you can't even make a complete sentence? Who is going to keep you from driving straight to Free People for retail therapy? Who is going to console you or strangle some sense into you with that seat belt? You're gonna need both. Who is going to let you sit in silence or let you talk? You'd better know the answers to these questions before you choose the driver. That is the kind of friend you need. The Thelma to your Louise.

All the hard work had gone down months before. Fear jumbled up my brain, and my heart was like a tangled ball of yarn with no beginning and no end in sight. Just a big ball of mess. What am I going to do? I am a stay-at-home mom with no income. No one will hire me. I can't raise two kids without a job. I have no skills. I am a singer-songwriter, and we all know that inconsistency doesn't pay the bills. Where will we live? Oh, my God, where will we live? Not only am I taking down my life, I am taking down two children with me. Up to this point, I thought pushing out two beautiful eight-pound babies was the hardest thing I had done and would ever do. I was wrong.

I have to stay in this marriage. I am stuck. I am shackled, because I can't live out there on my own. Carrying the weight of this toxic marriage has to be easier than carrying out the fate of my family as a single mom.

By the time I had gotten to the courthouse, I was done emotionally. Totally and completely done. Emptied out. I didn't want to fight with him anymore. I didn't want to struggle in my marriage anymore. The thing that nudged me through was envisioning a better home for my children. I would daydream about the other side of all this drama. A home where parents didn't fight all the time. A home where we had peace. A home where I was putting food on the table and clothes on their backs. A home where we were all thriving. Even their dad. The positive thoughts of surviving pushed me. Excited me. Those thoughts plus the encouraging words from friends gave me the energy I needed to keep pushing for what I wanted. Out.

Name a doubt. I had it. Name a fear. I owned it. I thought of every possible terrible scenario that should make me stay. I felt incapable, unqualified, and underrepresented. When I didn't have a drop of strength left in me, I would sit behind my keyboard and just pour it all out. It got ugly. It got snotty. I found myself writing about all of my disappointment in how life and marriage had turned out. Those piano keys have caught many tears, and they have helped me express many feelings that I otherwise couldn't speak.

Recently, after my show in Augusta, Georgia, I received an email from an audience member who said she just came to the show to laugh, but what I shared about my divorce had the most impact on her. That night, I sang "This Ole Radio"—a song I wrote about the long drive out of Colorado back to Tennessee. I was forty and moving back in with my parents in my hometown with my kids for some emotional rehabilitation and to get back on my feet. She said in her email, "I am preparing myself to leave my marriage of fifteen years." It was all too familiar. I knew exactly where she was. And now my story was her metaphorical getaway car. I was someone who had been there, done that, in every sense of those words. I had walked the hard steps. I had started over with hardly two nickels to rub together. She needed to hear what my "now" looked and felt like. She needed to hear what is possible on the other side of the pain and struggle. She had the strength; she just might not feel it right then. She needed a little hope when she thought all she wanted was my humor. She needed to know how to push the gas pedal.

But this isn't really about divorce; this is about the moment that I realized I CAN DO HARD THINGS! We can do hard things. You can do hard things. You have the strength within you to do the one thing you think you cannot do. One step at a time and one job interview at a time. You have it in you. And when you don't have it, your friends stand in the gap, wait in the getaway car, and remind you of your truths. They remind you of the alternative. They remind you of why you started fighting for it in the first place. I couldn't wait on the resources or the "right time," because I would have been waiting forever. The only resource I needed was desire. The desire wiped the tears from my eyes so that I could see to take the next step. I didn't know where I was stepping, but the desire for a new life was just poking me until I moved. Forward.

I had to repeat these words to myself often: "What lies behind us and what lies before us are tiny matters compared to what lies within us."

And if Ralph Waldo Emerson said that his obstacles were TINY MATTERS in the 1800s, when indoor plumbing and electricity had yet to hit the market, then I am pretty sure you can overcome your obstacles, too! That means that the power within your heart, soul, and guts far exceeds, outweighs, and overshadows any circumstances of yesterday or tomorrow. Do you believe that? Can you believe that for just one second? Just long enough to stare courage square in the eyeballs? Can you believe it long enough to step one foot into the court-house or rehab facility or doctor's office? Can you believe it long enough to go start a better life?

Now that I am seven years removed from this story, I have the hindsight to understand that leaving was only 5 percent of the *hard* that staying was. Once the fear released its grip on me, I could see the freedom I was able to attain. I did it. And I fought the guilt and shame the whole stinkin' way.

I don't know what your tipping point is. We all have different struggles. And maybe your *hard* includes reconciliation and staying for something beautiful. All I know is that you are far more resilient than you think. You are going to survive to tell about it. And I hope you will tell about it. Other women (and men) need to hear about that one time you didn't think you could hold your head up. They need to hear about those bills that you couldn't pay and the checks that bounced. They need to hear about the prayers you whispered over your children while they slept and you wept at their bedside. And if you experience a speed bump in this journey, get up and remind yourself of the strength within you. Define the boundaries again and again if you have to. Define what it is that you will not tolerate any longer. Decide what the "other side" is going to look like for you, and determine the steps to get there. You may have tried plan A and plan B, but there are twenty-four more letters in this alphabet to try.

I am living proof that God's protection and provision are a solid foundation on which to cast your cares. I am proof that anything of value is worth the work. Sure, you'll be tired and grow weary. Sure, you will have to take steps forward without knowing exactly where to place your foot. Bet on it. People will come along on your journey and bless you. People will come along on your journey and make a place for you. People will speak truth. Some people won't, and some people will judge you, but that's OK. You take the high road. You take the road that leads to your freedom. And you'll take the people with you who have encouraged you along the way.

One day, you'll have enough of your own strength to drive your own getaway car. You'll have the strength to pick up your heavy shoes, push your own gas pedal, and squeal your tires with a hope for new beginnings. And the day you do, those friends who once drove the getaway car will be standing in the rearview mirror waving at you as you drive yourself into your new horizon.

12

A TIME FOR EVERYTHING

Is there a face serum called "Before I Became a Mom"? If so, sign me up to be on your multilevel marketing team. Make me a believer. Time is not the friend of my tanning-bed-withered body. My sun spots say, "I have been there and done that, around the block two times over." I am a sun lover. If you can't tone it, tan it, right? I used to choose who I dated based on whose mom owned a tanning bed. It was a major player for me. Don't hate the player, hate the game. And as time passes, the exhaustion, overtanning, bad diet choices, and bad men choices are telling on me by way of wrinkles. Time is telling on me.

The only things that are certain in this grand ol' life of ours is death, taxes, and the passing of time. Time can heal us, time will change us. Regardless, time will give us facial pleats, but I prefer to call them laugh lines. Call them what you want, but I didn't get these lines by laughing. I got these lines from sleepless nights with two children. I earned these lines. But that doesn't mean I have to keep them—let's be clear. Life is full of contrasts. It takes us through mountain peaks and valleys, ups and downs. But age is the great equalizer. Age is the price of wisdom. The world keeps on spinning, and somehow we keep turning with it.

Some of y'all have a hard time grasping this time thing. I, too, have an issue with it, because I'm rarely on time for anything. I get it honestly, though, I really do. I lived in Colorado for five years, and every time my dad called me, he asked, "What time is it there, Heather? It's five here, what time is it there?" Every durn time. "Dad, I am an hour behind you, always and forever. It's been five years. I'm still in the same time zone, get with the program."

I feel like I should also mention that I was out this morning and saw that someone in my neighborhood still has their Christmas decorations up on Good Friday. Excuse me, but if you still have your Christmas decorations up this close to Easter, we need to talk. Just because that wreath on your front door turned brown doesn't mean the rest of us can't see it.

Christmas is not supposed to just roll right into Easter like Jesus rolled away that rock at his tomb. What are you gonna do? Hide the Easter eggs in stockings "hung by the chimney with care, in hopes that the kids would find Easter eggs there"? I mean, we are about to celebrate the resurrection, and you still have Baby Jesus hanging out with the Wise Men on your front lawn. The Wise Men are long gone by now. And I saw you moving those reindeer so you could mow the lawn—how about you let them fly on into your attic until next Christmas? I hate to blow up your theology, ma'am, but the birth and the resurrection were a solid thirty-three years apart. We ain't waiting thirty-three years for you to pack up your Christmas decor.

Christmas decorations at Easter is like me celebrating my anniversary six years after my divorce. Celebrating Christmas this time of year is like having someone throw me a baby shower for my sixteen-year-old. *Also, I'm registered at Game Stop.* I would rather watch Cousin Eddie empty his septic tank on my front lawn than look at your Christmas lights year-round.

What I am trying to say is, there is a time for everything. A time to hold on and cherish and a time to let things go. Do you know how to hold on and cherish the moments that should take your breath away, or are you rushing to take a picture of it and share it for everyone else to enjoy more than you? Take some advice from Pam on *The Office*: take mental photos. Commit them to your brain. Make a conscious effort to cherish. I think somehow that makes a neurological pathway to your heart. And what are the moments that matter the most to your heart? The small, intimate minutes that make your soul sing? You'll never regret the moments you spend with the people you love. You will, however, wish you had been more aware, more present.

When I was the parent of small babies, I loved every minute of it. I truly tried to the best of my ability to live inside of each and every single moment. I was alert and aware, and I don't even know how except for Jesus. This is not everybody's early parenting story. Some of you live in the hell that is baby prison, and you wish to God you could get out. I dreaded the day my kids would get big, drive a car, learn to talk back. I wanted to hang on to their littleness as long as I possibly could. And I did. And now they're big. And now here I am at another seasonal crossroads. Learning to let go.

Letting go is always the hard part, I know. It's not easy for anyone. If you need some motivation, take a trip down any country road in the South this Saturday. My speck of the world is filled with people who don't know how to let go. And it's evident from the fourteen broken-down vehicles in their front yards. We hang on to everything! I've got one word for you, sir. Just . . . NO.

I've been a people pleaser most of my life. I've done what I think I'm supposed to do to make the people around me happy. It took me a hot minute to realize that yes was a choice, and no was also a choice. And dang it, I live in America, where I have the freedom of choice. But yes was my addiction. I had to learn how to make myself a priority. Needless to say, my own happiness was pretty low on my list of priorities. I haven't said no much in my life. I thought I would be happy when everyone around me was happy, but after years of struggle, I finally learned that making everyone around me happy is completely impossible.

Trying to constantly please people keeps us from cherishing our moments—because we give OUR moments to everyone else. I don't know about you, but I want my mental photo albums to be full. I want my memories of days gone by to encourage my seasons ahead. I reference my divorce quite a bit because I said no for the first time in my life and had to walk in the consequences of that no. That no unlocked chains that had bound me for years. This no was my yes. And for this people pleaser, that was huge. It was time. The time had come when I had to make a choice. It's like time showed up like the Grim Reaper, and I couldn't avoid it any longer. Your time deserves a confident yes and a confident no. You deserve your time to show up and be seen.

Time is many things. It's an equalizer. A bridge. A healer.

Have you ever hurt so deeply for so long and beat yourself up with the thought that you should be "over it by now"? Pain takes time. We can't expect ourselves to rapidly heal from assault and the trauma of loss and just get on with life as it used to be. There is no instruction manual on the time it takes to heal. Some wounds are deep, and some wounds are wide, and we're all different. Some wounds may never heal. Time gets all mixed up. The smallest thing can trigger a memory, and there we are, living our past life. We all heal at different speeds, physically and emotionally, but time can be gracious to us, and time will allow us to live and breathe again.

Wouldn't it be great if the promise of healing and wholeness came without the pain? What a life! But what if the promise is IN the pain? What if the greatest gifts and perspectives of your life come from the pain you experience? I am living testimony of this truth. My shattered marriage was necessary pain.

I would have never found myself. I would have never found my voice. I would have never found my future.

In the summer of 2018, I was bearing the weight of my aspiring career as a traveling circus clown (comedienne). It had been a crazy few months. I had written my first book, been to Haiti, released my debut country album, and gone on a multiweek comedy tour. I broke away for some time with some close friends and my kids on the beach. My kids played, and I lay on the beach like a dead person for seven solid days. The only sounds I cared to take in were the waves, the seagulls, and the indie vibes that were playing in my ears. My plan was to read a book I'd had on my radar for ages, but when good music is playing, I have to stop and soak it in like a sponge, so I didn't make it past page 9. I also reached the height of what I would consider remarkable parenting status, as I barely ever knew where my children were the entirety of the time. About once an hour, I would try to wake myself from my euphoric state to look around and see if I noticed their sunburned shoulders bobbing in the water, in the hopes that surely if they were drowning, someone would've told me.

As I lay on that beach, day after day, my mind played the old tapes of my old normal, and I marveled at how one ac- cidental video now allowed my heart room to breathe. I felt the vacancy in my life where fear and worry once staked their claim. I remembered where I was and how I felt when I was fighting the war and compared it to how I felt in that very moment: at peace. I remembered the struggle and the cycle and the anxiety of doing it alone, and I remembered you— the one who's still in it. The one who doesn't see a light at the end of her tunnel. The one who will most inevitably come out the victor but doesn't know it yet. You—the one who is choking back the tears as you read these words that sit heavy on your chest. The one who cries herself to sleep wishing and praying for any kind of breakthrough. The one who cries for time to speed up and take the pain from her. The one whose baby has spit up on her new shirt and just wants to go back in time to when she had sleep and sanity.

I lay there in that sand crying for the seasons past and for the pain that almost took me down. Those tears felt as heavy as lead. My friends and I soaked up the sun and the love and the reality that we were finally in a place to do something for a single mom—if only for one right now, at least that's something. "Let's give somebody what we once needed. Let's love. Nothing in return. A total stranger." And in that conversation, we decided to use my platform to send a single parent and her children on vacation.

Hear me—this is not about me and my ability to give someone a beach vacation. And this is not some sick display of false humility or some manipulation tactic. I don't want your attention or your accolades. This is a testimony of time that has passed. I was that woman who never thought I would ever be able to take my kids on vacation again. I would never have the money for that. I was the one who barely knew where money for the next grocery run was going to come from. The space between that pain and my toes in the sand was where all of the change happened.

You may not be in the pain right now, but I bet you know someone who is. You may not be able to give away a beach vacation yet, but I just bet you can give something. I bet you can give a hug or take someone to lunch or listen to someone's story over coffee. I bet some of you can help turn a single parent's lights back on or buy someone's groceries. Opportunity will likely come to you each and every day. And it will look you dead in the eyes and ask you if you're ready—if you're willing. Willing to look foolish, to break routine, to lay down pride, to give selflessly in your own time of need. And you get to answer. You get to choose. But let me promise you this: if your answer is yes, your reward will most definitely be greater than your sacrifice. When your head hits your pillow at night and your heart is pure and full of peace and empathy and your conscience is clean knowing you loved well that day, that is the ultimate reward. It's not the size of the gift you give. It's the heart behind it.

And to those of you who are still in that season that you think will never end—the ones who want to love but can barely love themselves, the ones who are crawling through the valley right now—know this: Your knees will not be muddy forever. There is a clearing and a light, and one day you will stand up, and it will lead out. Your TIME will come. You are not finished. Don't let bitterness and resentment hold you under water. Throw your head back, tell it no, and show it who you are. Show life and everybody in it that you will love in spite of circumstance. With everything in me, this is what I believe: there is a time for everything and these are the seasons we are made for.

Ecclesiastes 3:1–8:
There is a time for everything,
and a season for every activity under the heavens:
a time to be born and a time to die,
a time to plant and a time to uproot,
a time to kill and a time to heal,

a time to tear down and a time to build,

a time to weep and a time to laugh,

a time to mourn and a time to dance,

a time to scatter stones and a time to gather them,

a time to embrace and a time to refrain from embracing,

a time to search and a time to give up,

a time to keep and a time to throw away,

a time to tear and a time to mend,

a time to be silent and a time to speak,

a time to love and a time to hate,

a time for war and a time for peace.

13

ENOUGH IS ENOUGH

When I bought my home, I fell in love with the painted brick and board-and-batten shutters. I couldn't wait to move . . . except for the whole moving part. I'm tired just thinking about it. If the packing doesn't make you want to eat pills, the paperwork will. The home-buying process is just two papers shy of negotiating with the devil himself. Am I signing to own a home or handing over all my assets and the authority for my Realtor to resuscitate me upon cardiac arrest? Who even knows? Either way, I love my house. The second-best thing in my home, besides the people whom I share it with, is the giant pantry. I can walk in, do the two-step, and choose my favorite sauvignon blanc out of the wine fridge in one fell swoop. If that kind of pantry doesn't make you happy, there is no hope for you.

Welp, today I am nursing a battle wound that happened when I was reaching high for a roll of toilet paper on the top shelf and knocked a two-liter of A&W Root Beer off a shelf onto the top of my foot. The cap shot off and spewed sticky, high-fructose corn syrup all over everything in said pantry, including me. I was left bleeding (and dripping) right there on the pantry dance floor.

I have everything in this pantry. I have paper products, every type of pasta they make, no fewer than 189 canned goods, kale chips from 2012, and party supplies for every occasion. Everything I need for Y2K or a natural disaster is in this pantry. It is too risky to run out of ketchup in my house, so I have six bottles. I have platters and ice buckets for all the festivities. All of my dry baking ingredients are properly labeled in case *Southern Living* pops in for a photo shoot. I have old appliances that I only use once or twice a year. I have extra bags of chips and cereal boxes galore.

I wish I could pick up one of those cereal boxes, but they are all sticky and smell like root beer.

No one in my family even drinks root beer.

I live within five miles of Costco and eight miles from

Trader Joe's. When I am bored, you know where I go? It ain't the gym. I wander up and down the aisles of that giant box store, and it takes my hard-earned money two hundred dollars at a time. My strawberries may be organic, but my money sure ain't. It doesn't grow in my backyard.

I have a lot of weaknesses, but I do have one strength: my pantry. I am always stocked, never without. A life of abundance (at least in the form of canned goods). This is the way of the suburban family.

Once when I was in my twenties, I visited a friend who lived in the heart of Brooklyn. We spent the weekend shopping at vintage stores and eating pastries at ungodly hours of the night. It was urban and delightful and simple, and I wanted to quit suburban life and move myself into her 367-square-foot home. She commuted five days a week into Manhattan for her job at Fox Sports. But once she was back in Brooklyn, she walked everywhere and lived within one square mile of her neighborhood. Her grocery lists consisted of ingredients that came from the market on the first floor of her urban apartment building. She knew every employee's name in that store. She knew exactly what aisle her ingredients were in. A quick trip, in and out. If they didn't sell it, she didn't need it. She made one purchase at a time for one meal at a time. She didn't need all the cabinet space, because she didn't have all the cabinet space. She had one set of dishes. One set of glasses. One jar of spaghetti sauce, not four. One box of pasta, not every shape. I found myself a little jealous of her slim living. How was it possible to live in the middle of every possible resource and not need it all? And, like, why did she not even have sugar for sweet tea?

In the South, we believe that simple living means being close to nature and far away from concrete. We believe that simplicity is found in wide-open spaces. We believe that running out of food for guests would be the worst possible scenario. Our motto is "We would rather have too much than not enough." If we ever ran out of cupcakes or sausage casserole at a baby shower, we could potentially have to move to a new town and start a new life.

But my friend's Brooklyn life trumped my beliefs. It was simplicity at its finest. No big trips to the grocery store, spending hours loading, couponing, scanning, unloading. One bag toted up the stairwell, and dinner was well on its way.

When was the last time you took a gander at the yogurt aisle in your local grocery store? There are at least three hundred kinds. Do I get Greek? What about Jamie Lee Curtis's yogurt that makes me poop? And what kind of sociopath buys unflavored, unsweetened yogurt? I don't even know, but I am fairly certain we aren't friends.

Don't even get me started on the hundreds of mascara options. Have cosmetics companies run out of adjectives to describe our lashes yet? Bold, undeniable, sensational, plentiful, voluminous, colossal. If I could have back all the time I've wasted on these unnecessary choices, I could've invented my own mascara.

STOP IT, ALREADY. I just can't take all the options anymore. The menus in restaurants are twenty pages long, you have to be an engineer to listen to music, and I can't work my television remote. When you check out at a store, the cashier asks you a million questions. *NO, I do not want loyalty points for this one pack of Bubble Yum. Swipe it, take my cash, and let me out of this jail.*

I miss the days of going to the local video store and choosing a tape for Friday night. Do you remember the process of elimination? It was a simple one. You spent time holding hands with your date, strolling those aisles that smelled like teen angst and Cheetos. And how did you choose? Easy. You chose the tapes that were not rented yet. Now, between Netflix, Amazon, and Hulu, I have hundreds, if not thousands, of movies to choose from. I am up to my eyeballs in movies and have no clue what any of them are about.

What's it gonna take to say no to all the excess? Solitary confinement?

Maybe just a heck of a lot of discipline.

Maybe a redefining of our beloved American dream.

In spite of my overflowing pantry, I actually crave simplicity. I can't stand the chaos of busy. I never sold my children into the slavery of competitive sports. I never volunteered to be room mother. I know my limits. I enjoy a slow Saturday morning at home in my sweats with a good cup of coffee way too much. The world around us will take what we give. The world demands more busyness, more money, more opportunities, more tasks, more more more. And my heart runs the other way. While I am glad I have flavors of toothpaste from which to choose, do all those choices make our lives better? Are we any happier today than we were fifty years ago with the quick, individual-sized microwavable options? Are we happier in 2,400 square feet than we were in 1,000? Are we happier because we have more options? I'm not convinced.

I am a mom, which by nature means the temptation to overcomplicate things is strong. We want to do all the right things and provide all the opportunities for our kids. We don't want them to go without. Earlier this week, my son asked me for thirty dollars for a pass to a haunted house. Right. So, what I am hearing you say, son, is that you want me to give you good money to walk into your own bedroom down the hall. Is that what I am hearing? What's the difference? Your room already looks like the thirteenth realm and smells like death. You can't walk in there without tripping over something. If you will give me a minute, I will put on a mask and jump out of your closet and scare you. I'll just pay myself thirty dollars.

It's conversations like this that make my children think I am the meanest mom on the planet. They've never earned a single penny and have no clue how long it takes to earn fifty dollars on minimum wage. They don't know what great lengths I will go to in returning an item that I haven't opened just to get $1.12 back into my checking account. They have no clue that we eat dinner at Costco because it's the cheapest pizza in town. They just think that Mom really loves the cheese pizza.

See, I have a responsibility to set the standard for what simplicity looks like in our day-to-day lives. We don't have to have it all. I want to teach my children about the simple place where our pocketbook, our calendars, and all the "stuff" in our homes reflect our family's convictions and values. Stuff is not important. People are, and I want them to enter adulthood knowing that. But the intersection of good intentions and reality is a four-way stop in a one-horse town. I have to help them navigate. Mostly because I love them. Also because I don't want them to end up on an episode of *Hoarders*.

Before you close this book thinking I am some hippie-dippie who plans to live in a tiny house, think again. I am not jumping on that bandwagon anytime soon. There is no amount of money you could pay me to live in a hot box of teenage farts and body odor. I am not selling my car to traverse across town on a Schwinn ten-speed. No to that. It is hard to imagine life without the modern conveniences of my front-loader washer and dryer.

I like nice things. I would rather buy one really nice pair of jeans than five cheap pairs. As I have gotten older, I appreciate quality much more than quantity. But buying a brand name because it is in the magazine or on my screen—sometimes it's tempting. I can quickly have boxes of clothes stacked up for a garage sale if I am not careful. This was my story just last year. I purged the excess of my overblown closet into sixteen bins of Marie Kondo bliss. I was proud but mostly mortified.

Ashamed that my leftovers could've clothed a small village. It was my wake-up call.

I remember the first time I took my daughter to the bowling-alley arcade. She played games to earn those little tickets to buy those little pieces of crap toys. What costs forty-three cents in the beginning cost eighteen dollars in the end. Playing the games was the point. Shopping the loot was what she loved. That glass case filled with crap was the cheap, little-girl equivalent of me every time I shop the home-decor section at Target. We can't decide, because there are so many options. SO MANY OPTIONS.

I died a thousand deaths waiting for her to choose between a sucker ring and a glow stick. By the time she was done, my skeleton could be found on the sidewalk bench. And we all know how this story ends. She didn't pick either one. She chose that little pack of M&M's because she is my child. That expensive little pack of chocolate candies gets her every time. It should be so easy to just pick one and move on, but she wants it all. We want it all.

Aren't we all that little girl peeking into that glass case? Peeking over our neighbors' fence? The more options there are, the more disappointed we are by what we can't afford. The upgrade of leather seats, the shiny new boat parked next to our old clunker, the new refrigerator with all the bells and whistles. It steals our joy. Nice things are great, but if we're not careful, they can rob us of our joy and gratitude. Sometimes it's best if we just don't walk into Best Buy. It's best not to stroll through that car lot. Maybe for some of us, it's best if we avoid Black Friday to stay home and love our people instead. (Let's not get crazy.)

What I'm finding is that with simplicity comes improvement. We may just have more time for people when we stop rushing to keep up with the Joneses. We may have more time for the ones we love when we reduce the amount of laundry we have by reducing the amount of clothing we buy. When our calendars don't allow time for relationships, we have lost our way. When we only buy what we need and what we can afford, our hearts get lighter and our health improves. When our burdens get lighter, our sleep gets deeper. With less of the unnecessary, we can find what we are looking for: time and rest.

What if we stopped chasing the next best thing? The best thing is probably already in front of you. The best things can't be bought, and we know it. But we fail to live like it. If I only allow those things that are beautiful and useful to dwell in my home, I can set the stage for a well-lived simple life. To move from meaningless to meaningful might be our greatest life's work. To fill our lives and our homes with only what fills us up from the inside. I should always be uncluttering my soul, making room for the important stuff and getting rid of the stuff that collects dust.

Always remember, if you find yourself peeking over your neighbors' fence because the grass looks greener on the other side, it's probably fake.

14

HAPPINESS PREVENTION

I'm headed out to see some friends tonight, and let me tell you what we are not gonna do: we are not going shopping on this tax-free weekend. I realize that it's back-to-school season and everybody is trying to save a dime. But, literally, that's all you save, a dime on a dollar. Even less. I am not fighting crowds to save a few dollars. In fact, I will send you a few dollars to stay home with me. I would rather lose a limb. There is nothing that I need that bad. Saving those few dollars is not enough to overcome the sheer rage I would feel when dealing with those crowds. I will not trade my happiness for a few dollars. It's worth far more than that. And please don't invite me to go shopping when we are on vacation. Exploring an outlet mall in a beach town is a terrible use of time. Sand, sun, water, piña coladas around every corner, and you lunatics want to rummage through reduced-price clothing at the durn outlet mall. People who go shopping on vacation are pure psychopaths. Shopping with hordes of people is work, not a hobby. No, thank you. I will be keeping my happiness and maybe finding some new friends.

You know what else steals my happiness? Someone who is all up in my personal space. And besides church on Sundays, shopping on tax-free weekend is a surefire way to have people all up in my business. We all know someone who has no boundaries when it comes to personal space. I am all about having a conversation, but you are gonna have to back it up, mister. Why do you have to get nose to nose with me? Who are you, Floyd Mayweather? You challenging me to ten rounds? If I can see the fillings in your lower right molars, you are too close to me. Back away.

Here's another thing that prevents my happiness: public restrooms. Can we talk just a minute about the filth that we are subjected to when we have to pee in the food court at the shopping mall? Why are the latches on the stall doors ALWAYS broken? Can the great inventors in this world not figure out a foolproof latch that will last? We can put a man on the moon, but we can't build a door that stands up to wear and tear?

And who invented that toilet-paper holder that doesn't spin? As if the chintzy, frail quality of the one-ply wasn't enough, "let's put it on a spool that doesn't fit and make them work for it while pee is dripping down their legs." And for the love, the countertops by the sink are always wet. I would set my purse in a pile of cow manure before I set it in that sopping mess, much less on the floor. Public restrooms need to put hooks on the edge of the countertops for women to hang their purses like bars do. And the smell of public-restroom cleanser is enough to make anyone gag. Especially in airports—and I spend an awful lot of time in airports. And to top it off, the smell of public-restroom hand cleanser screams at you the rest of the day. Barf. And because I loathe those air hand dryers, I always choose the paper-towel dispenser. There we all stand, waving our arms around like idiots, trying to get one square of a paper towel to roll down. The motion sensors on those things make any self-respecting adult look like a complete moron.

Here's another revelation I had later in life about something that steals my happiness. Social pressure. When someone invites me to hang out and I don't really want to, I feel pressure. Why? Why do I feel like I have to? Men don't understand this part of us girls. They just say no, without any emotional strings attached. But we girls are so scared of making someone mad. If they were really my true friend, they would realize that when I am home, I am on my couch under my electric blanket like an eighty-year-old, and I don't want to go anywhere. You can come see me, but I don't go out much. Unless I am on a tour bus and they make me.

I believe we have to fight for our happiness. And I believe it is worth fighting for. We have to protect it and tend to it like a garden—down on our knees, pulling weeds that try to grow and choke it out. I think that happiness starts with loving yourself enough to be true to what makes you happy. No one is going to pursue those things that make you happy for you. It is about waking up and deciding how you are going to spend your twenty-four hours, how you are going to tend to your happiness garden—what soil and nutrients will make your crops grow, what will make you bloom.

And sometimes you just have to fake it until you make it.

What are the things that make you happy?

Here are the things I love: authenticity, real relationships, truth, justice, chocolate, and donuts. I love my children, my people, good coffee, good cheese, good music, Joanna Gaines, and Jesus. And I have learned that if it doesn't fall into one of those categories, it probably needs to go. Trim the fat. You have to do a happiness inventory often, because that list can change with the passing of time. Assess the parts that are preventing the happiness and say 'bye, Felicia.

Even if you are pursuing happiness, you won't necessarily always feel happy. For example, I can sit on my couch with PMS and not feel happy about it, but I can create an environment where I am more likely to be happy. I can create a space where I feel safe and secure, comfy and cozy, and mostly that space is filled with chocolate.

When I'm unhappy, I have to take inventory and identify what is blocking me from experiencing the fullness of life. I have to dig deep and identify the source.

Do I have unrealistic expectations for myself? Of somebody else? Am I stressed? Why? Do I have a conflict in a relationship? And how am I coping? What am I doing to pull myself out of my slump?

Can I be honest? For me, shopping is what pulls me out of a slump. Spending money I most certainly don't have for a temporary fix. There, I said it. And then there I am, on the floor of my bedroom with all these really cute Anthropologie shopping bags, and I have blown it. The nonexistent budget is blown. I am pretty sure I didn't need these clothes, but I sure wanted them. So there's the thief of joy right there. Not

Anthro—it's not their fault. The store that smells like sage and fresh lilies gave me a moment of euphoric bliss, but at the end of the day, my lack of self-control and my urge to "make myself happy" by buying a thirty-dollar candle and a bohemian maxi dress only adds to my downward spiral.

There's been a lot of talk about social media stealing our happiness and replacing it with dissatisfaction and depression. But social media is just a platform. The behavior of the people is the common denominator. Social media is also a platform for sharing good things that make us happy, like the good ol' 30-Day Thankfulness Challenge. Let's see just how much "thankfulness" we can publicly cram into a single month's worth of Facebook statuses. I actually love reading these posts. While some folks are as sincere as the day is long, there are some folks who run out of thanks fairly early and start praising Jesus for ridiculousness somewhere around day 4. That, or they turn their "thankfulness" into passive-aggressive ways to air their dirty laundry.

"I'm thankful today that my baby daddy got arrested. He got exactly what he deserved." That's a little extra, but you get the point.

Sometimes our view of gratitude gets a little skewed. Ann Voskamp challenged me as I read her book, *One Thousand*

Gifts, to dig deep for the gratitude. It's not always in the obvious.

Early on in life, I set out for the American dream: the perfect (dysfunctional) family, the white picket (chain-link) fence, two perfect kids (nothing funny here; my kids are perfect), a (slobbery, allergy-prone) dog, a nice (extremely used) car, and a (lean) 401K that was being built while I stood back and did all the things I loved—raising babies, making music, and making a home. Absolute perfection (per fiction).

After many years, I actually achieved some form of that delusion, so my thankfulness looked something like this: "Thank you for this beautiful life you've given me. Everything looks exactly like I hoped it would (minus the happiness and the fence). I really appreciate that. Also, I would greatly appreciate you keeping it this way from here on out until I enter your pearly gates with thanksgiving and into your courts with praise. P.S. You're doing a great job, Lord! Keep up the good work!"

This sounded completely acceptable to me. It's all I knew. Thank Him for the obvious (even if you are failing miserably and wearing a disguise). Make everybody think you've got it all together, Heather. Pretend. And while you're at it, throw some "thankfulness" in during the month of November for good measure. After all, it's not called Thanksgiving for noth-ing. I guess somewhere along the way, with the Lord's fabu-lous sense of humor, He decided to call my bluff. "Thanks for the yearly shout-out, sweet girl. [This is Jesus talking, for all you slow learners]. Some not-so-holly-jolly Christmases are headed your way. Let's see what you've got . . ."

Years of perfecting the facade—it was a pretty good run, don't you think? I mean, the diligence, y'all . . . Little did I know the real Thankfulness Challenge was on its way. Straight out of divorce, I was faced with something nightmares are made of: no home, no money, no job, no direction, no stabil-ity. I was more than a thousand miles from my hometown. Would this hurt forever? The Lord used all of those things that were stripped away to show me all the "things" that actually mattered. As my journey progressed, my mind-set changed from "Thanks for all the stuff, God," to:

"Thank you that I get to hold my babies every night. Thank you that we are OK. Thank you for friends who gave us a place to stay. Thank you for peace in the middle of tur-moil. Thank you for support—people who didn't leave when things got messy, who gave me a job and money and a U-Haul and a listening ear . . . Even Christmas. Thank you that we are surviving. And most important, thank you for the hurt that has led me back to the cross. Thank you for the loss so that I could know what true wealth really looks like. Thank you for the mess and the uncertainty and the not-knowing so that I could watch you work and move and lead and do what you do best. Thank you for loving me more than I ever thought possible. And thank you for the broken things, because I would've never known just how beautifully you can put them all back together."

And I meant it—every word. I remember on more than one occasion saying, "God, if this is what it takes for me to feel close to you, I'll stay in this place forever." I'm really grateful He didn't listen to me on that one.

Life has its way, doesn't it, of bringing out the worst and the best—the blame or the gratitude? Trust me when I say I've had my days full of anger and self-pity. But I also found Jesus while I was at the bottom, and I hung on to Him for dear life. He showed me the beauty in the ugly and brought me more joy in the upset than I ever knew possible. He has given me more good comedic material through all my bad choices and life experiences than I could've ever hoped or dreamed. (Sometimes we have to laugh or we'll cry. Am I right?) He has taken the chaos and turned it into delight. And for that, Lord, I am forever grateful. Perspective is everything, isn't it?

Life is full of hard seasons. Know that it is OK to be where you are in your season—unashamed, unapologetic. Just know that somewhere in all that wreckage, there is a little piece of treasure begging to be held up and recognized as beautiful. It's there, in whatever situation you are facing, and I just bet you won't have to dig too deep to find it. I challenge us all to let the 30-Day Thankfulness Challenge turn into a routine benediction. And if you're the one with the baby daddy in prison and that's the best you can come up with, then you go, girl. You've gotta start somewhere . . .

15

GOOD-HEARTED

Decisions, decisions.

What in the world am I going to wear today?

Should I eat those two cookies for lunch or, like, a turkey sandwich on Ezekiel bread?

Should I go to that event?

Should I try yoga?

Should I say yes to that coffee date?

Should I start a podcast?

Should I be a comedienne?

This is my stream of consciousness from a random day last year.

So. Many. Questions. In so little time. It's no wonder I've developed a strong love for wine.

Some decisions are as clear as crystal. Others are as clear as my shower water after a spray tan. Some require much thought and deliberation. Others are no-brainers.

Let me throw out this disclaimer: THIS BOOK DOES NOT HOLD THE ANSWER. In fact, it may even confuse you all the more. What I can offer you, however, is companionship. You are not alone in your efforts to decipher the yes and the no, the should or should not. I get it. I get you.

Sifting through the sand to find the gold is an exhausting process, but I recently read a book that is helping me weed out the rocks. I have a feeling I am about to be judged harshly, but do your worst, I don't give a . . . crap. The book: *The Subtle Art of Not Giving a F**** by Mark Manson. I'll pause here for you to process the fact that I consciously purchased and read the entirety of this book knowing its title—and content, for that matter—involves a curse word. We good? OK. Moving on.

I love people. I value other people's ideas and thoughts, and I love to please. I know these are good qualities to have, but sometimes I have a tendency to lose myself. Sometimes I get so concerned with what everybody else thinks about me, wants me to do, or believes is best for me that I forget to do what I want to do. I become robotic and beaten down—not by other people but by my own sentencing. When I succumb to the will of well-intending others and lack the gumption to speak up for myself, a pathetic lie of total dependence circulates in my brain until I have convinced myself that I am a victim when, in fact, I am not.

Case in point: "I am so miserable since I've gained ten pounds. Eating on the road is killing me. I can't get it off."

LIES.

Miserable? Yes. Eating on the road is killing me? MY CHOICES ON THE ROAD are killing me. I can't get it off? Umm, no. I CAN get it off. I've gotten it off about a million and one times now, and I can do it again. This is where I tell all you sweet people NOT to send me ideas for weight loss. I don't care. I'm already on it. Thanks in advance. I digress . . .

This is the type of repeating tape that has played in my brain over the course of my whole existence. It is the fight, the struggle, that each one of us has to win. Apply it to anything and everything that offers confusion and creates a victim mentality in your life. It's valid. And it's not about the weight loss or the thing. It's about us.

I have been frustrated lately about the lack of control I've felt in my own life. Work, play, weight, the skin damage I've created from my excessive consumption of sunshine over the past three decades . . . you name it. But yesterday, after completing the entirety of Mark Manson's book, I had an epiphany. I am giving way too many "craps" about way too many things—about the wrong things. I'm giving so many craps, in fact, that I'm talking myself into believing the lie that says I have no control over my life—that I am but a victim. That's enough to overwhelm even the likes of Brené Brown.

When I finally sat down and said, "What's bothering me?" I took mental notes and asked myself, "What in this situation can I change?" And guess what? In almost every situation, there was something I could do to change it. Not happy in my marriage? I can change it. Not happy with where I live? I can change it. And guess what else? For a few things I could not change, I could still alter how I viewed and responded to that situation. I don't know if I can get enough laser treatments or slather enough cream on my sun spots to make a difference. It doesn't matter. The question really is: will I try anyway?

What will my attitude be? Just how many craps will I give? What's important here? Who is important here?

In answering these questions, do you know what I found? CONFIDENCE.

And guess what else I found?

ME.

Ahh . . . here she is. Here's that girl who cares about the important things, who lets the less important fall away, and who believes, above all else, in herself.

Here I am.

I am not a victim. I am in charge of me. I am in charge of my life, my brand, my attitude, my outfit of the day. I am not incapacitated by change or hurt or fear. I can be. I have been. But I refuse.

With this rebirth also comes the burden of knowing that I will make wrong choices and that with those choices come responsibility and consequences.

Noted.

The fear of the wrong choice can be gripping. I have lived with it, and it tries to wrap its hands around my neck frequently. But every time I pry away its claws, I remember who I am. That I am strong and capable. Capable of making mistakes but just as capable of owning them. Equally, I am capable of making good, sound decisions and humbly owning the fact that I have what it takes to continue doing so.

I may not have the ability to open every door or bucket-list my way through every single day of my life. But I do have the ability to make my own way—to see what's coming and to know whether or not it's a door I want to walk through. I have the ability to choose.

To wear the thing (or not).

To go to the event (or not).

To do the podcast (or . . . yes, I'm doing the podcast).

I also have the ability to decide how I will see the things I cannot control. Some things are not of my choosing. Some things that are for the good of the whole aren't always the things that feel best to me. But I still have a choice. And in case you were wondering, so do you. You have a choice in how many craps you give and what you're giving them to.

You have the capacity, the bandwidth. You may feel overwhelmed, but you are not.

You have it in you to reprioritize, to shift, to start over. You have what it takes to think logically and live practically and love graciously. You have what it takes to love well—to be good-hearted. This is where I always want to stay. This is the book I want to write: "The Subtle Art of Being Good-Hearted." That's not nearly as good a title as Mark's book has, but it's the story I want to tell.

16

TALK IT OUT

I am perched in a public-restroom stall with my purse and shopping bags hanging on the back of the door grazing the top of my head, minding my own business, when all of a sudden, I hear someone talking to me.

"Excuse me?"

No response. I'm assuming she needs some tissue. She could also be having a heart attack. I don't know.

"Do you need some tissue?"

"Mmmm-hmmm."

After carefully wadding up Target's one-ply for my new friend, I reach my hand under the stall to give her this toilet-paper life preserver, but she doesn't take the bait. She does, however, keep talking.

"Mmmm-hmmm. That's right."

OK, girlfriend is either having a stroke or having sex, and I don't want to be around for the outcome of the latter.

I hear a flush. Peeking through the crack of my stall door, I see that little flashing blue light on her ear. Are you kidding me right now? She has been on the phone the whole durn time she has been pooping in the Target bathroom. At least she washed her hands, I guess.

What have we become? Look, I understand what it is like to pee in peace. For a decade, I had a child under my feet every time I went to the bathroom. But people, if the person on the other end of your phone call wants to talk to you that badly, they need to find more friends.

I am an external processor. I have to sort out all my feelings with my mouth before I commit them to my heart. I have to state the facts, plead my case before a jury, and maybe I will have enough emotion left to then communicate with the other party who is involved in these feelings. I have to survey those closest to me to process. I have been like this since I was a child. People like me figure out the answer as they hear themselves say it. Surprisingly, we may not even agree with what comes out of our mouths. We are just trying on the words to see how they fit.

I have sorted through my feelings about life over many cups of coffee and phone calls with close friends. But you know what I ain't gonna do? Sort out my feelings in public on my speakerphone with all of God's creation to hear me. Innocent bystanders.

Nobody wants to be hearing about your bunions, lady! And I could've lived three lifetimes without ever knowing that they had to scrape the inside of your mouth for a sample. Although now that you mention it, whatever happened with that?

And look, girl, I am so proud that your husband is trying to change and get you back. I am super glad to hear that he just passed his recent drug test. But if you don't get him off your speaker, I'm gonna need the name of his drug dealer. I do not need to know all of this about you or his employability. Some things are meant to be discussed in private within the four walls of your home, not the four walls of this bathroom stall. Now, zip up your pants, wash up, and be gone. But wait! Before you leave, whatever happened with that? How will I find out the results? Can we exchange numbers so I can get the rest of this 411, because now I'm invested. And you have done this to me. You have invited me to lunch and then asked me to get up and leave halfway into my chicken salad sandwich. I didn't even get dessert!

My science textbook said our tongue is the strongest

muscle in the human body. I know this is true because some of y'all could enter a bodybuilding contest with that tongue flappin' of yours. And on speakerphone, no less. Y'all may as well stop going to the gym to work out your other muscles, because your tongue is setting personal records every stinkin' day.

Ma'am, do you work out?
Why yes, yes I do, I let my tongue do all the heavy lifting.

Who am I to talk? I can answer that. I make a living flapping these jaws. I sing and talk to put food on my family's table. (I just don't do it in the bathroom stall.) I admit that sometimes I talk too much or say the wrong things at the wrong time. And sometimes it ain't pretty.

See, it is my professional opinion that all relationships are built on communication; therefore, all relationships are torn down with miscommunication. Wouldn't you agree? How many situations could we have avoided or minimized if we had just said the right thing or kept our mouths shut? And why does that last part have to be so hard?

I spent fifteen years in a marriage where communication was always at the root of the problem. We both have advanced degrees in the language of sarcasm. Most of the time, our convos were patronizing, condescending, and indirect and rarely lined up with the image we portrayed outside of our home. Have you ever seen the meme that says, "Controlling my tongue is no problem, it's my face that needs deliverance"? Well, I need help with both. My tongue and my face are going to tell you how I feel. I can't hide it. It's a blessing and a curse.

It is also my professional opinion that women in general are prolific communicators. There are many exceptions to this rule, but in general, we do not have any issues with letting you know how we feel. In case you didn't know, I am a daredevil, and overcommunicating is my extreme sport. Some of you are also placing first in this category. It has been my experience, however, that men are ranking low in this sport.

Even though we are fully aware that men like to keep things easy, answering her question with "OK" is never a sufficient response to anything. It's just not enough. All of our questions should be answered like the essay part of an SAT— not the kind of test that Aunt Becky cheated on, the real kind that gets you a scholarship. Complete, thorough, and accurate answers. We want an essay. A dissertation. An exegesis.

And ladies, what you have to realize is that your man is simple. He really is. Don't overcomplicate things. Don't expect him to read your mind. He may be struggling to read the instructions on a box of macaroni and cheese, much less be able to crack the code to your tangled web of a brain. You have to say what you mean and mean what you say. It's that simple. And if you are sarcastic like me, you have an additional rule: say it without an eye roll. It's harder than it sounds.

There is a fix for all this, though. If you want your man to start communicating more, you can teach him how to say exactly what he means. For example, when he says, "Just go buy yourself what you want for your birthday," do it. Go to your local car dealership and ask to test-drive a new black Range Rover. Show up at his office in that car, and tell him you bought what you wanted like he told you to. That'll get him to show a little more interest.

I have a theory that men and women would probably last longer in a marriage if they didn't have to cohabitate. Think about it. By the time you were moving out of your parents' home at eighteen, everything they did drove you crazy. Think about if you had to live with your parents now. Well, I did it at the age of forty, and it ain't for the faint of heart, I'll tell you that much. Why? Communication. It's harder the longer you LIVE with someone. Now, please don't rush out and tell your significant other that I told you to go rent an apartment. It's just a theory. I am no research psychologist. I ain't no Brené Brown. It's just a simple observation. Maybe we should start building compounds made of those tiny houses, and you buy them in a set of two. Maybe the *Sister Wives* know something we don't. I'm taking notes.

Regardless of where we cohabitate, we have all been guilty of putting too much pressure on a significant other to meet all of our communication needs. They can't be all that. We need friends, we need counselors, we need mentors who will listen. And we need chocolate.

For those of us with a tendency to overcommunicate, sometimes we need extra reinforcements to help us know when our time is up. We need help in the event that we need to cut ties with people we have loved or people we have invested a lot of time in. People like me always have one last point to make, one last sentiment, or one last jab. But there comes a time when no contact is the only contact a girl should make. No texts, no posts, no likes on Insta, no nothing. A gag order. A moment of silence. Keep it shut.

Girls, you need a friend who will threaten to take your phone away. You need a friend who will secretly delete the number of the person you need to avoid. You need a friend who will take your phone and click "Block Caller" when you aren't looking.

King Solomon in the Holy Bible said that death and life are in the power of the tongue. We have been warned. And that's quite the responsibility we are carrying around. Perhaps the self-control some of us have to really strive for is not saying no to ice cream. Perhaps reining in our tongues is the kind of self-control we should work to achieve.

Controlling your tongue doesn't mean you shouldn't speak up for your values, morals, ethics, or justice. Controlling your tongue means that how you say it is more important than what you actually have to say.

If I've learned anything, I've learned this: where there is drama, there is also manipulation. I've been in some relationships that were nothing more than cheap, poorly acted daytime dramas without the face-lifts. Some of the lead roles should have won a few Emmys for their fireplace mantels. Most of the nonsensical drama and manipulation was rooted in a struggle for control.

I spent so many years feeling misunderstood and confused about what I really said versus what people heard me say. Two very different things. Instead of learning how to talk better, we need a few lessons in how to listen better. The wise King Solomon also says, "To answer before listening is folly and shame." Again, with all the wisdom there, Solomon. Listening could have saved me many heartaches along this journey. When people feel heard, they feel validated. When people feel unheard, they revolt. When children feel that their parents aren't listening, they misbehave. When spouses feel unheard, they shut down or escalate. When minorities feel no one is listening, they kneel or march. When women feel unheard, we start a freaking revolution.

When is the last time you looked online at comments under celebrity posts on social media? Have you ever seen such disgusting behavior? Have you ever seen such vile words spewing from the mouths of humans about other humans? You don't even have to look at a celebrity's page. Just look at mine. Maybe those hateful trolls on the Internet are just searching for their voice. Just grinding and snarling to feel heard. People often ask me if I get upset about negative comments on my posts. People ask me if I worry about those people's opinions. And to be honest, I couldn't have handled these comments five or ten years ago. But when you go through loss and come out healthy on the other side, you aren't really threatened by the opinions of others who mean absolutely nothing in the grand scheme of your life. My family, my friends, my faith. Those things are important; the rest is just showbiz, baby! I am a big girl now, and I can handle it. And when I can't, I have a person for that.

To engage with someone and to let them know that they are understood, we have to offer our ear. Offer our best intention of hearing them. When is the last time you had a conversation with someone who had very little in common with you? When is the last time you engaged someone who had a different political perspective or religious perspective? When is the last time you offered your ear to a person from a different generation and tried on their shoes for size? When we learn to walk a mile in another's shoes, we gain understanding that has power to change our lives.

Listening does not mean I will agree with you. Listening is the best way to show respect and humility. Listening means that I am willing to understand you. If Jesus can sit with the woman at the well and listen to her, I think I can listen to my man explain why a wired Ethernet connection is faster than a wireless access point. Listening also means not thinking about what you want to say when the other person is talking. Oh, snap. Have you ever been around someone who is calm when discussing tense matters? Or someone who tilts their head gently to one side when they don't understand you? I had a boss like this once. She was so calm and so wise. And we were on opposite ends of the spectrum about matters of faith and politics. I learned so much from watching her communicate. Actually, I learned a lot by watching her listen. Her body language told me that she heard me. I knew that she wanted to understand my perspective. I can only hope to be that kind of listener. To give life not with my mouth but with my ears.

Have you ever been around someone who constantly speaks encouragement? I have, and I have wanted to punch them in the face. How can you be so positive? How can you find the silver lining in everything? But you know who I loved to sit and talk with? You wanna know who gave me life in little doses every day in the workplace? Yep. Her temperament and personality, so different from mine, gave me life. Her words were so careful and thoughtful, and I craved to be around her. Her positivity was contagious.

The tongue also has the power to give life through forgiveness. To forgive and set someone free isn't for the other person. We know this. Offering forgiveness gives freedom to me, the perceived victim. And regardless of which side you find yourself on, or which side the other person thinks you are on, the tongue has the power to give life with the words "I am sorry." Again with the humility thing. Three little words that can bring so much freedom to a heart. Most of us Southern ladies learned to start our insults with "I am sorry, but . . ."

I am sorry, but that girl fell off the ugly tree and hit every limb on the way down.

That is not what I am talking about here. Stay focused.

The simplicity of saying "I am sorry" means you value the relationship over your ego. Even if the relationship no longer exists. It is possible to forgive someone and never have a conversation about it with that person. (*Gasp.*) For real? Me? An external processor can forgive and set someone free without talking about it? Yep. When it is sincere and whole, you can save the drama for your mama. You don't need the convo, you just need the freedom. You just want the deliverance.

Forgiveness is such a beautiful thing. When I remember God's love for me and who He says I am, I am finally able to put shame in its place and walk in the freedom God has called me to. Without forgiveness, you'll hit a brick wall. Shame had no place on my journey, and I was the only one allowing it to come along. We are human, and we make mistakes. But the authentic love of the Lord was never earned by me in the first place. Why do I think I get to keep it to myself?

My mouth has gotten me into trouble. You don't believe it, but it's true. It has made me look stupid, and now my mouth is making me a living. I am not sure what that says about my self-deprecating condition or what it says about my fans, but my mouth makes people laugh, and I hope that gives life. My mouth has also set my heart free. My mouth has offered advice and offered grace. My mouth has stood up for injustice, and, as of late, my mouth has fought for my own future. Sometimes finding the right words requires you to find the right feelings long in advance. Sometimes that takes time. In the waiting, it is OK to be quiet. It is OK to not speak, not jab, not ridicule. It is OK to not be right. It is OK if others have opinions about your silence. Let them. You are responsible for you. I am responsible for me. We don't have to ever agree to show respect or humility. Talk it out. Or don't. Either way, communicate.

The single biggest problem in communication is the illusion that it has taken place.

—GEORGE BERNARD SHAW

17

BETTER NOW

A man once said that drinking is just stealing happiness from tomorrow. I don't know who that man is, but I bet he's never had a Moscow Mule in an ice-cold copper mug. I am not a big drinker, but I do love mimosas. I used to be a prude. I was always the designated driver. If you had one drink, you may as well be a drunk. I had marked you with a scarlet letter and was praying you through rehab. I have learned to relax a little bit in the last few years. And by learning to relax, I mean I have also learned how to take myself less seriously.

I am a survivor of Bible college. It was a weird place, where I was to ignore the opposite sex; we were forbidden to share side-walks because that is where sexual immorality begins . . . on a sidewalk. No mixed bathing (in a swimming pool or in the ocean). No jeans. No flip-flops. No form-fitting clothing. No skirts or shorts above the knee. We all know that promiscuity starts with a glimpse of the kneecap. Two more inches up, and you could have seen my Mormon undergarments. Don't even think about dancing. The only dancing we did was the spiritual version of *Soul Train*—a "Jericho March." The only touch that happened between sexes was during prayer meetings. And if there was a cute boy, I pretended to "need" more prayer so he could lay a hand on me.

When I was eighteen, I left home on my maiden voyage to Pensacola, Florida. Eight hours away, with no cell phones and a car with 217,000 miles on it. It was my intent to never return. Someone in my church paid for my schooling, and I am forever grateful for their generosity. But I am not thankful that I left college thinking that separate sidewalks were totally normal.

Most teenagers straddle the fence between their parents' faith and the ways of the world. I did not. I never dipped my toe into rebellion or curiosity. I walked the line. Rules and "the forbidden" were all I knew. It's all I chose to know. I didn't want the weight of "sin." I believed that any white lie, any lack of discipline in my Bible study, the mere thought of a cuss word, must be repented of over and over, and then

I must repent for not repenting enough. Every night, it was my goal to list my daily sins. God forbid I fall asleep with my headphones on before confession. As soon as my eyes would open the next morning after a night of nonrepentance, I let out a sigh of relief that I was not smote in my sleep or plagued with boils on my face for an unrepentant heart. If I did not burn up in the fires of hell that day, I had to carry yesterday's sins over to the next night's prayers. That's a lot of millstones around my neck. Psalm 139 was meant to be an encouragement to me; instead, it scared me more than having to return home. If He knows when I sit and when I rise, He must know about the impure desire I had to be kissed by a boy. For shame. There was no end to the cycle. There was no peace. There was no rest. Just shame. And for what? God forbid I actually acted on a thought I was having. I aimed for an unattainable level of holiness. The more I followed the rules, the more righteousness I could obtain. The more "freedom from sin" that I harvested, the more fruitful my life would be. Well-meaning adults turned scripture into man-made prophecies.

Most people at my age are sprinting to enjoy this thing called life. I am just now learning how to crawl. I guess with age comes a little bit more freedom from our childhood construct. Lord, I've sung enough worship songs about "walking in freedom." But I am sorry. I lied. I didn't know I was lying. My definition of freedom was inaccurate. I thought freedom looked like perfection. I thought living in man-made rules about pleasing God was freedom. And if I struggled, that was the punishment. The weight of disobedience on my conscience was the penance.

The Oxford English Dictionary defines freedom as "the power or right to act, speak, or think as one wants without hindrance or restraint." And if you look at that definition, that did not represent ANYTHING I knew about freedom. The idea of "power" in and of itself is powerful. But the "right"? In my religion, the freedom to question anything was not an option. It was disobedient and wrong. In some strange way, we idolized the punishment. The fallout. The backsliding followed by the redemption. That is when we felt most justified.

I was very genuine in my religiosity. I was very tender and loving and authentic in my pursuit of righteousness. While I was busy trying to have freedom from my home life, I didn't know I needed to be free from myself. Until a few years ago, when I started meeting people who didn't grow up this way. They looked at me with confusion in their eyes. They looked at my anxiety and burdens with skepticism. You mean everyone doesn't live like this?

Somewhere along the way, I confused my behavior with God's nature. His goodness was dependent on my behavior. There was no mystery. I could define everything about who He was in my life and how I was to approach Him. I was a ton of fun to be around. I judged everything and everyone through the lens I used to judge myself.

I was tired and unhappy. I didn't live a life of grace and mercy. I sure didn't extend it to anyone else. And this road ran out when I needed grace the most. I pushed the restart button. My faith finally became real. My faith became separated from the practice of religion. My faith was what I woke up with each day. It was the only thing that kept me going. My faith was actually what made me start asking questions about what I really believed—the questions about what I believed and what mattered that were typically "off the table" for discussion.

I finally decided that I did not want to live this way anymore. I no longer wanted to be the Christian who judged and criticized everyone. We are the worst. We will take down our own just to be right. We will isolate and betray just to "honor God." That is not OK. Because we will all need grace one day. We will all know hurt. We will all know loss. And what we won't need in those moments is rules. The rules won't help heal your heart or anyone else's.

I have found that small-mindedness is not synonymous with being a person of faith. And I am choosing to walk in that realization. My goal is not to be better than anyone else but to be better than I used to be. To live with eyes wide open—aware of the hearts and hurts of those around me. To extend dignity in circumstances that I do not understand. To allow others to choose their own way (as if it's mine to allow), even if it is not a way I would choose.

I can't get along with anyone who looks at life differently. I can't have a conversation with someone who might buck my system; because my way is the right way. Can I encourage you to evaluate how you treat people who don't believe the same way you do? What are your opinions about them? What are your misconceptions about them? I promise you have them, because I did.

When you realize that people have misconceptions about you, too, you can start knocking those walls down. Put down your shield and sword. Stop the fighting, and start loving. I'm pretty sure that is what we are supposed to do.

18

HERCULES

The year was 1988. I was twelve years old, entering seventh grade, teasing my bangs, and wearing Hammer pants. And he was . . . actually, he wasn't.

Not yet.

Not until that December.

Then he was.

He was born.

I joke in my stand-up set and in my last book about dating a younger man, but in my defense, this has never been a conscious "thing" for me. I am not a cougar. Eww. Gross. Stop.

I have always "dated my age" or close to it. I have not always, however, dated my IQ level. I did not set out looking to date someone younger. If you do, it's you for it, as my granddaddy used to say. No judgment here. It's just never been the way I've taken.

Until now . . .

For almost four years postdivorce, I had only two loves in my life: my son and my daughter. I was 2 million percent devoted to a fault and felt at the time that their little hearts and minds had no room for anyone else. They had zero bandwidth and even less for understanding how or why they should have to welcome a total stranger into our lives after a trauma like the one they had experienced. I knew that they would not be able to piece together a life of stability with Mommy dating, so for me at the time, it was a nonoption.

Next to having to live with my parents for three months when I was forty, dating again was the weirdest experience of my life. I had no clue how or what or when, and the idea of having to learn just about made me want to eat glue. I decided to give it a go, but the constant fears of getting something stuck in my teeth at dinner or having to potentially kiss somebody good night after a date made me take a dating break.

Enter comedy life.

The year was 2018.

I was going on the sixth month of my comedy career—traveling three to four days a week, working on my set, doing stand-up for the first time in my life in front of total strangers. My manager decided it was time to tour, whatever that meant. Tour required a team of people with fancy job descriptions who would critique my performances, help me hone my set, design a stage, and then present me with an overload of information until I cried, so that I could be successful, of course. Included in this group of important people was a production manager named Stephen. I met him in May. He came to my house with my program director, Pepper, to present his ideas for my set design. He set up his slide show and talked about all the things he had been working on, and I'm sure it was all really important.

I wouldn't know.

All I knew was that he was way cuter than this Power-Point presentation he was trying to show me in all his professionalism.

"Thank you so much, Stephen. This has been so insightful. Speaking of sight, your eyes are maybe the most beautiful I've ever seen. And so dark. Can you see into my soul with those things? Can you tell that I think you're cute? Please say no."

I knew he had to be every bit of thirty-five, which was well within my range. He was tall and dark and handsome and Indian and intelligent and kind and well spoken, so something under the surface had to be very wrong.

Well, there goes that.

They left, and I went on with life, and that's as far as it went . . . for a minute. I didn't think much of it after that. After all, there are lots of cute guys out there. It's gonna take more than some dark eyes and really good hair to make me think twice.

A few short weeks later, my team and I met in a Kroger parking lot in a town just east of Nashville to hop a bus and leave for tour. We, including Stephen, filled out all twelve individual bunks the bus held. We (they) loaded merch and bags and a million and one snacks, and at midnight we headed out and drove all night to our first stop. Even though Stephen was now a 24/7 part of my road life, my focus had shifted from my recent day crush to honing my comedy set and drawing the crowds. I was in awe of this team and this life, and I was ready to do hard work, weeks on the road away from my children. Sleeping in a bunk and not being able to use the bathroom on the bus should the urge hit me. There was a lot to focus on, so I didn't really have time to be thinking about much else. Also, I was grown and busy and professional, and there was no time for such shenanigans.

Night 1 of bus life was a huge, fun success. We all laughed and talked and ate and drank like we had been together forever. The next day, the crew unloaded, the team worked tirelessly all day, and I focused on the night ahead. It was a sold-out crowd in Louisville, Kentucky, and as far as I could tell, it was a happy one. I had somehow managed a two-hour show, and by the time I finished meeting and greeting and showering and the team had finished loading out, it was almost midnight.

We all hopped back on the bus and started what would be a nightly unwinding full of continual conversations, loud music, and games. These fools love them some games. This process lasted hours into the night, as most of us were so wound-up from the day's and night's events that we were able to decompress more completely in our family setting than in our individual coffin-beds.

Somewhere around night 3, during one of our late-night unwindings, I found myself next to Production Manager Stephen. We were all in the throes of numerous conversations and "Name That Musician" when he and I found our way into our own little discussion. We talked about all the things—people and travels and work and family and music. I was over his cute face but at this point was very much into his brain and his philosophies. He knew something about every-thing. He had sincerity and goals, work ethic and leadership. He loved his family and all of humanity, and his kindhearted-ness and desire to know me had my interest. It was hard to hear over the loud Broadway musical numbers and constant chatter, but I heard him loud and clear after I officially, in my grown-up forty-two-year-old voice, asked him how old he was.

"Twenty-nine."

"I'm sorry, what?"

"Twenty-nine."

"I thought you said twenty-nine."

"That's right. I'm twenty-nine."

TWENTY-NINE??? As in born in 1988, twenty-nine?

How is this even possible? Your receding gray hairline says you are every bit of thirty-five, and your knowledge of the French and Indian War and the way you religiously and care-fully take out your contacts and brush your teeth every night say you're all-day-long the internal ripe ol' age of sixty-four.

Except . . . twenty-nine.

Well, that solves that. It's been great talking to you, but since you are well under normal range, this conversation stops at global warming and skinny jeans.

Except that it didn't.

We talked late into the night, long after the rest of the team had gone to their respective cocoons. It wasn't awkward, because we didn't notice. We were busy laughing and learning and listening. We talked about movies and politics and culture and God and played each other songs we loved from artists we respected, and right at the moment when he played me that song by Martin Sexton, there it was. I looked at him, and he looked at me, and right in that moment, we both knew. And I could only think one thing:

Oh, crap . . .

This is a thing. He's twenty-nine, and I'm forty-two, and this is a thing.

I feel it. I can tell. This cannot be happening.

Not only was I graduating from high school when he was learning how to hold a crayon, but we work together! We live on this bus together, and this is not OK. Nope. Shut it down, girl. Don't let your brain and your heart run away with you. Stay in reality. Stay focused. On your career, idiot! Not on him!

Somewhere around five A.M., we exchanged good nights and a smile that acknowledged the awkwardness of this situation. We hopped into our bunks for what felt like a solid two seconds. I tried to sleep, but thoughts of the night and my excitement for him to get to see me first thing the next morning kept me awake for the duration. If our age didn't keep us apart, that would surely do the trick.

Except that it didn't. Day in and day out for two solid weeks, we talked during the day. We talked all night. We ate together. We worked together. We explored cities together. We were . . . together. Everybody knew it, and finally, we did, too.

To the outside world, this probably looked like straight craziness, but to us, it just made total sense. He was an old twenty-nine, and I was a young forty-two, and somewhere in there we just met in the middle. We just needed to see about this thing. It was a risk, but it was a risk we were willing to take. I had two kids and a divorce under my belt, and *are you sure, dude? Are you sure you even want to explore this? If you don't, I understand. You can cut and run at any time.*

If you knew how many times I offered and how many times he declined, you would love him, too.

He just wouldn't leave. My thinning hair and sun spots just sucked him in. Days turned into weeks, but not without me offering him escape routes. Weeks turned into months, and on August 23, 2018, sometime around 7:32 P.M. Paris time, right there in front of the Eiffel Tower, he told me he loved me and that he had loved me since Little Rock in June. And somewhere around 4:41 P.M. Paris time on November 20, 2019, he told me again as he got down on one knee in that same spot and asked me to be his wife. This guy is everything I never knew I needed and everything I hoped was out there. And for the first time in my life, I feel exactly like I never have but always hoped I would. Happy.

Our relationship is one of the sweetest experiences of my life. It is not hard or burdensome, but that doesn't mean we don't have differences. We have an obvious age gap, but don't let it fool ya. He falls asleep at 9:00 watching CNN, and I want to stay out late and have fun. His family is from India. Mine is from Redneckville, USA. He is brown. I am white. He is frugal. I like to shop. He is intentional and sensible. I live in my feels. But even though it may seem like there are reasons we shouldn't work, there are a hundred more reasons we do. Besides the fact that I am obviously a picture-perfect partner, he brings a few things to this table, too. Besides your basics that should be staples in every good relationship, he also taught me how to eat rice and yogurt with my hands, and folks, that's something money can't buy. I have also been offered other invaluable gifts that I do not take for granted.

Honesty.

Respect.

Stability.

Health, and not just the physical kind.

Loyalty.

Fun.

Patience to work out old wounds.

Safety to heal. To fail. To try new things.

Strength.

Tenderness instead of rage.

Partnership in place of control.

Admiration.

Encouragement.

Room to unpack any leftover baggage.

Family. His—the ones who pull me in and love me in
   spite of my history, and the ones I love back and
   call mine.

He challenges me and makes me think. He listens to me.
He disagrees with me. He believes differently from how I
do about certain issues, but he lets me be me. He values my
thoughts and my opinions and my life. He's real and genuine.
He loves my children. He teaches and listens and guides. He

cares about other people. And he invests. In himself and others. In me.

He thinks I'm beautiful without makeup. He loves my cooking and always thanks me for my efforts. He mops and vacuums and dances while he does it. He never says a bad word about anybody, and when he tells me how much he loves and appreciates me, he means it. Please know that he also puts his pants on one flat foot at a time, OK? He is not perfect. He gets frustrated and anxious, and one time, he didn't really like the fish I cooked for dinner, and he let me know about it (rude). But he is my match in every way, and I would rather listen to him tell me all about 4G and the new Apple Keynote than to ever be without him.

Despite everything I've just written, I'm not here to fluff him up. I'm here to fluff YOU up. I'm here to tell you that good men exist. Good women exist. Good partners exist. They may not come packaged the way you think they will. They may not be old enough or pretty enough or smart enough, whatever that even means. They may wear skinny jeans and talk too much about the electoral college. But they're out there. If you will work on getting yourself healthy, I believe that person will come your way. They always say it's when you least expect it, and I think they're right. You may find the love of your life and the greatest risk you've ever taken sitting on a tour bus next year. You may fall in love in Little Rock and say "I love you" under the Eiffel Tower. You could very well be writing your own book next year all about how you're just as much in love today as you were the first time you saw him. I don't know. You may be the happiest you've ever been, alone, just you and Netflix. And that's OK, too.

But here's what I do know. Your future is bright. God has not forgotten.

I'll end this chapter with one more mushy thing, and then I promise to move on. I have written a lot of songs about loss and heartache. This past year was the first time I wrote about love and happiness. Stephen loves the constellations, so I surprised him with a song. I wrote it with our friend Blessing Offor. I hope when you read the lyrics, you'll remember that not knowing what's ahead isn't a bad thing. The love of your life could be wrapping cables and working on a PowerPoint just around the corner.

Hercules
Yeah, I've got some baggage
I'm scared that it might be too much
But you just keep unpacking saying

"Girl you know I'm strong enough"

Now, we could go to Paris

Yeah, we could go around the world

I'm acting kinda careless

That's 'cause you make me feel comfortable

I used to see you only in the sky, Hercules

Now you're next to me

Now you're next to me

I used to see you only in the night, Hercules

Now I can't believe how *bright* you really are

Now I can't believe how *right* you really are

Now, I don't know the future

But I know it belongs to us

I'll spend all of my time

But what it buys will never be enough

I used to see you only in the sky, Hercules

Now you're next to me

Now you're next to me

I used to see you only in the night, Hercules

Now I can't believe how *bright* you really are

Now I can't believe how *right* you really are

ACKNOWLEDGMENTS

I would like to thank you, the fans and readers, for your friendship, your loyalty, and your ability to take a joke.

To my partner, Stephen. You are my perfect match and the absolute perfect blend of love, tenderness, and constructive criticism. Thank you for loving our family and coming along for the ride. You're more than I could've ever hoped for.

To my kids, as always. You've made me so happy (and a little fluffy around the middle).

To my team at Chandy Group. You guys keep the machine running, and I'm grateful to have you in my corner.

And my deepest thanks to my friend and cowriter, Heather Lenard. Thank you for helping me put thoughts on paper, but mostly thank you for loving me through the process of finding myself. You are an amazing writer, but most important, you're what true friendship looks like.